The Art ~~of Selling~~ Rocket Science

Book 1
Building a Sales Program for Technical Services

CHARLES MCINTYRE
and
HAROLD GLASER

Copyright © 2014 Charles McIntyre and Harold Glaser
All rights reserved.
ISBN-13: 978-1496103321

CONTENTS

ACKNOWLEDGMENTS

We are grateful for our families,
colleagues, and clients, and we acknowledge that we
learned everything we know from them.

i

Chapter 1
Introduction: The Art of Selling Rocket Science

"The jungle is dark, but full of diamonds."
- Arthur Miller, from <u>Death of a Salesman</u>[1]

> *We were leading a marketing meeting at one of our firm's offices. Sales had been meager for the year, so we were trying to build enthusiasm for developing new business. An engineer who'd been in the company a long time stood up and asked, "Isn't it enough to simply do good work for our clients? Why do we have to SELL all the time?"*
>
> *We had heard the question many times before. In theory, doing a good job, getting your calculations right, and delivering satisfactory results should be enough to assure success.*
>
> *"Have a seat," we said. "Let's talk about this."*

The practice of selling consumer goods has been a mature profession for many years. A large body of knowledge has been developed and shelves of books published on strategies to sell products such as beer, toys, or clothing. Business owners hire legions of trained sales people with marketing MBAs to successfully sell their products.

Sophisticated sales techniques have also been developed for more complex goods. While a consumer might be easily convinced to buy one brand of tortilla chips over a competitor's offering, sales strategies are quite different for persuading buyers of fighter aircraft or mainframe computers.

What has been ignored, in our opinion, are publications or teaching curricula based on the sale and marketing of services, especially technical services. We have worked within the highly technical engineering and scientific industry our entire careers. We have long realized that few

---

[1] Miller, Arthur. Death of a Salesman. New York: Penguin Books, 1986.

books have been written specifically for sales and marketing of technical services, though the sector employs millions of people in engineering, architecture, applied science, information technology, management consulting, and niches within law and finance.

The Challenge of Selling Technical Services

A major challenge inherent in selling services is their abstract nature. Services cannot be touched, and are therefore regarded by buyers as intangible. A great book on this topic by Harry Beckwith explains much by the title, *Selling the Invisible*.[2]

Another fundamental challenge of technical services is that the "selling" is usually performed by the people who also provide the service, rather than by a non-technical sales force common to other industries. A chemical engineer can more convincingly sell chemical engineering services to another chemical engineer than a salesperson who isn't trained in chemical engineering.

It is paramount to keep in mind that as recently as 25 years ago, many technical professionals conducted almost no formal sales and marketing activities because they were unneeded. Business from new clients was won by word of mouth, and repeat business from clients was a reward for technical quality and good customer service. The very thought of sales was

> *In this book, we use some terminology repeatedly and sometimes interchangeably:*
> - *Business Development (BD)*
> - *Marketing*
> - *Sales*
>
> *We could split hairs over their definitions, but in our minds, they are equivalent. Moreover, we personify them as job labels. These terms refer to individuals active in these roles, which can overlap with other jobs, such as:*
> - *Engineer*
> - *Scientist*
> - *Consultant*
> - *Technical Professional*
>
> *Because this book focuses on the world of technical professional sales, we have tried to keep things simple by grouping roles together. Keep in mind that no matter what you're doing today, the origin of your education and experience, or the path upon which you find yourself, you are ultimately reaching a common (and rewarding) destination-- the selling of technical professional services.*

---

[2] Beckwith, Harry. Selling the Invisible: A Field Guide to Modern Marketing. New York: Warner, 1997

considered unprofessional, reserved for used car salesmen. A large number of these technical professionals who did not formally market their services remain in the industry today; many have a great deal of influence in their company's operations because of their seniority.

But those times are over. We have built solid careers, along with our colleagues, supporting the marketing and sales of complex, technical services. Some of these services are literally **rocket science**, distinctly different from simpler consumer services. The professionals who provide these services earn their livings by developing solutions to complex problems, or inventions that meet their customer's needs.

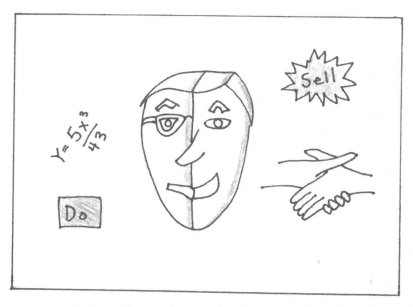

To us, the most fascinating aspect of selling technical professional services is that it consists of two very different components, both of which are critical. The first part is the technical content, familiar territory to engineers and applied scientists, based on their schooling, experience, and often their personality.

However, the second component of selling technical services is the emotional side, relating to values, feelings, and human psychology. To many practitioners, this side can be foreign and uncomfortable because they received almost no education or training in dealing with people and their emotions. However, it is a critical component of success, because we find it common in our business for a decision-maker to not fully understand the technical details of their own project. Technology is often so complicated that buyers resort to other factors to make decisions. Frequently, these are emotional, outside the technical world. Because of the human factors in making buying choices, we contend there is **art** combined with the selling and buying of **science**.

We're fascinated with this marriage of *rocket science* and *art* because their union creates a contrast between highly technical professional services and the human side of how people make choices. Hence the title.

Intended Audiences

We wrote our books to offer insights to four interrelated audiences that are critical in business development:

- Technical professionals, mainly engineers and applied scientists
- Marketers working within these types of firms
- Managers of technical professionals and marketers
- Clients buying from technical professional services firms

Although your firm may be current in its approach to marketing and sales, we're willing to bet that you have more than a few engineers or scientists who have never formally learned how to directly sell their services to clients. If you are new to selling (or buying) within the technical services world, we offer plenty of new ideas for developing your approach. If you've been around the block, hopefully we can teach some new tricks and improve your game.

We also find that many technical professionals believe that selling requires classic, heavy-handed "sales" techniques or late-night schmoozing. In modern professional technical services, this could not be further from reality. Because of the need for accurate information from the client, being a good listener is more important than being a good talker, or schmoozer. Slick salespeople turn off customers, whether they're selling services or used cars.

If you're a marketer, we offer some unique skills for coping with, if not excelling at, what you do. How well you relate to technical professionals will depend greatly on your ability to understand not only the rules of the market, but also what makes technical people tick.

Managers will find that providing oversight of your sales force of practitioners is different from being able to win work yourselves. It's also very different from controlling results within their technical discipline. Managers are often promoted into the role either because they are successful technically or they know how to bring in new work. Neither quali-fication adequately prepares them for motivating and then directing the efforts of their peers in the world of sales.

If you're a buyer of technical professional services, we hope that by better understanding how the sausage is made, you can improve your ap-proach to working in the industry. Also, people can change roles during their career. Technical professionals can become clients, and clients can cross over to technical professional services. If you understand how your providers think and act, you'll get ahead, and stay ahead.

The Nature of Technical Professionals

It is important to understand the nature of technical professionals, their personality, and the way they think and act. Technical professionals are wired to reach the right answer. They have a knack for science and mathematics; slogging through data to reach solutions is embedded in their DNA. Unfortunately, when they enter the business world, they are forced to work with people (clients, colleagues, partners) who have prob-lems that do not always require technical solutions (schedule, budget, stakeholders, risks, value, politics). Also by nature, many technical profes-sionals (but not all) are introverts to some degree. They retreat to the comfort of their craft, keeping customers, colleagues, and bosses at a safe distance.

Fair or unfair, two other traits frequently stand out: they dislike change, and they are not commercially minded. These mindsets can place them at a disadvantage in becoming successful at sales. And support team members and managers will work uphill to make progress with them. Fortunately, we offer advice and tools that have been proven to work with a range of personality types, and a methodical marketing process that lev-erages the natural abilities of technical professionals.

We contend that by understanding the strengths of technical profes-sionals, and their weaknesses, you can improve the sales process in your organization. Throughout the book, we keep returning to this point: by breaking down the mystery of sales into task-oriented methodology, the art of sales can be transformed by the rationality of science.

Guidance for Marketers Working in a Technical Environment

For non-technical marketers reading this book, we offer empathy, advice, and tools. We have never seen a firm where marketing is in control of the business; it is always a support function. As a result, this requires skills that are based on reason, logic, influence, and charm to get technical professionals to do what needs to be done. Most marketers will not be able to tell a technical professional what to do; to be successful in sales, and in their career, marketers must therefore be *influential*. This book will teach you communication skills that promote persuasion, and will arm you with compelling arguments designed to appeal to our practitioners.

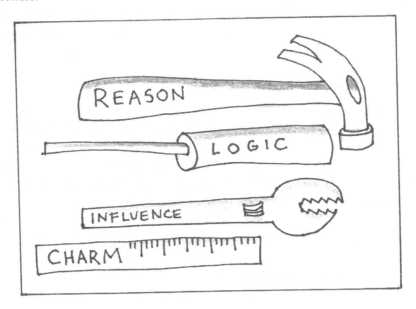

Understanding Sales Will Put You in the Driver's Seat

Of course, if one were to stay in a role that was purely technical, that's just fine with us. No doubt, there is a need for outstanding technologists. However, even strictly technical staff will have contact with customers, if only in a support role. Our focus is to encourage technical staff to go beyond technical support and become directly involved in business development, because we believe it is an equally important aspect of the business. And those technical professionals who are multi-skilled (especially in sales) will be more valuable to a firm, which can be particularly important during tough economic times.

In the end, there's no better way to ensure that the projects you work on are interesting, even fun, than by taking control and selling your own services. If you're out of the office seeing clients, then you'll have the opportunity to determine the kind of people with whom you would enjoy working.

The case for being involved in marketing and sales is compelling. The reward for following the principles made in this book is a full plate of interesting and challenging projects. By thinking, planning and acting in ways that are beyond what your competition is prepared for, you will impress your clients and all those around you. This approach benefits not only yourself, but your company. If you point your feet in the right direction, march forward along the path we describe, and follow with your head and your heart, you can win the work to keep yourself and your colleagues satisfied.

Experience is the Best Teacher

Any discussion of sales will naturally encompass a wide range of topics. There are a lot of other books that establish solid foundations for sales techniques; we refer you to our favorites in the annotated bibliography. We don't attempt to reproduce the good work of other authors. As a result, we've taken the liberty of reiterating their points in order to focus on the unique challenge of marketing technical professional services.

We also did not conduct years of independent research to write this book. Rather, this is a book about what we do every day, and have done for many years. We have learned a lot from the great marketers we have known and observed. As you read our books, you will see that it covers the entire process of building, implementing, and continuously perfecting a marketing and sales program. We also provide real-world examples, successful tools, practical strategies, and everyday tactics for winning work in this highly competitive environment.

> *We stopped the marketing meeting in its tracks. "Look, let's answer our colleague's perfectly reasonable question, isn't it enough to simply do good work for our clients?"*
>
> *Unfortunately, we had to tell the engineer, "No. The competition has intensified because with the recession, clients have less work and more technical people who want to*

do it for them. We have to fight to win every project, just for the privilege of performing the good work we would like to be involved with.

"Moreover, when we manage to convince a client to hire us, they will expect that we will do a good job and get our calculations right. That's the status quo. They will also want excellent service from you, and also anticipation of their future needs.

"The biggest reason we need to actively sell our services is to control our own professional and personal destiny. If we attract clients and take good care of them, we'll be rewarded with increased business, in good times and in bad. The resulting profits will allow us to grow business as much as we choose, to add new staff, and to invest in new technologies and services."

Chapter 2
Being Smart is Not Good Enough – You Need Customers

"Should I try and be a straight A student?
If you are then you think too much."[3]
- Billy Joel, Recording Artist and Composer.

During my first week of work at an engineering firm, I realized my new employer was paying me to perform work for which I was not prepared. What a shock! Work wasn't anything at all like school!

I learned quickly that the bulk of the firm's assignments were in three areas: studies, design, and construction management. I was relieved to see that at least some of my "book learning" could be used on the job. I also found out that the veterans in the office could estimate an answer faster than I could plug numbers through an equation.

On the business side, I was even more clueless. I had no idea how we got customers, how much they paid for our work, or especially how these customers decided to award us work. I knew, however, that there was plenty of competition.

I got a real education on the second day of work. I was asked to perform a few simple engineering tasks. After confirming that I did actually learn something about hydraulics in college, I was instructed to stay within the budget and schedule. Huh? To me, a budget was learning to stay within the available cash in my wallet. And a schedule was my listing of classes. Now I learned that my work had to be done for $5,000 or less, and that I had three weeks to get it done. That was ten times more money than my first car. And a three-week deadline sounded like a cushy assignment.

---

[3] Joel, Billy. *It's Still Rock and Roll to Me*. N.d. CD.

A few days later, I was invited to another meeting for a different project, which had a budget of $400,000. I learned two things: (1) that I had to manage my time between these two projects, and (2) that $400,000 could be spent a lot faster than I could imagine.

I learned that our company had been selected for this work over a handful of competitors by submitting a proposal and attending an interview. When I asked if we were the lowest price, I was told in a stern voice, "We don't compete on price. You wouldn't buy brain surgery based on the lowest price, would you?" These early teachings confused me more than enlightened me, but the nature of my own naiveté proves our point-- there is almost no teaching about business basics in engineering school, so most technical professionals show up for work without a clue.

Education in school focuses on fundamentals and theory. Practical knowledge builds after schooling, with on-the-job experience. Perhaps, if your family were merchants or business-owners, then you might have learned practical business knowledge just by listening to conversations around the household, or by hanging around the family store. However, we're guessing that many of you were caught by surprise when you entered the work force as a technical professional or marketer with little background in business.

A brief review of some fundamental points is helpful for placing the rest of this book in context. In looking back on the earliest days of our own careers, understanding these few basics would have helped jump-start our knowledge of more complex marketing and business development concepts.

Review of Business Basics

- <u>What is the one thing all businesses need to survive</u>? There are a lot of responses to this simple question. You might say a business plan, people, capital, a great idea, technology, or even hard work. While all are important, we contend that some businesses can survive, even be successful, while missing one or more of these ingredients. But the one thing a business cannot do without is customers.

- <u>Your employer is in business to make money</u>. Quite often, people say that their company makes car parts, or sells groceries, or builds highways. But the overall point of their business is to make a profit, at least in a capitalistic economy. Profit is a return on investment to shareholders (owners) of the firm. Over the years, from time to time, we have heard of individuals who have openly questioned the need to make a profit. Losing money over time will put you out of business. Profit allows investment; remember that on your first day of work you were an "investment," one that your company hoped would eventually pay off.

- <u>Your Company and your Customers make choices—lots of them</u>. We are fond of saying that life is full of little choices. One of the simplest examples is the need to make a choice between two equally attractive opportunities to win new work from customers. Sometimes we choose one over the other, and sometimes we choose to pursue both. Less frequently, a choice is made to pursue neither. The activity of making choices, and the information which forms the basis of those decisions, is a major emphasis of this book. Actively making good choices, based on knowledge and experience, may be the most important activity in being successful in business.

- <u>Customers want both your book-based knowledge and your practical experience</u>. It is important to appreciate the convergence of both your academic knowledge and on-the-job training. Customers buy both. Accepted practices or "industry standards" are important in knowing the "right way" to approach a challenge. Risk management depends on this line of thinking. However, the role of innovation in applying industry standards, especially as part of the sales process, becomes critical to competitive differentiation.

- <u>You work in a competitive environment</u>. Are your competitors nice people with whom you share war stories over glasses of wine? No! They're slugs to be crushed. Of course, you may temporarily work with these slugs in teaming situations, and you might even change jobs and work for them. But, remember, if you don't win, then you don't eat. Do you think the competition is sitting in their war room plotting schemes to be nice to you? Of course, not. They're scheming to eat your lunch!

- <u>Being smart is not good enough</u>. There is a lot more to knowing how to "run a business" than being in command of the technical aspects of the company's services. You might be, or may become, a great technical expert. But if you don't know how to convince customers to give you work, it will be difficult for you to be successful. Fear not, it is perfectly all right with us for you to "stay technical" and avoid the business aspects. Your company needs strong technical people for a lot of very important reasons. Customers certainly desire your technical expertise. But we have found that the most successful combination of skills is in individuals who blend outstanding technical ability with above-average sales and marketing talent.

How Does Your Company Win Work?

If your business is fast food, your customers seek you out. If your business provides a technical service, the transaction can be more complex. In most cases, your firm's business is based on transferring technology or knowledge, and you typically win work in one of the following ways:

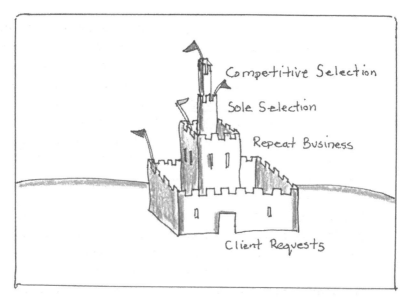

- <u>Work walks in the door</u>. This is the simplest method for obtaining work. Similar to consumer goods or basic services, the customer contacts you. They may already know you, or have heard about your work. Quite often a favorable referral from a satisfied client is all it takes. Your phone rings, a new customer is on the line. They have an unmet need, and they ask you to perform a service. You negotiate a contract, and your firm is off to the races. This happens all the time, but rarely often enough to grow a company.

- Your company has previously worked for a client. Sometimes, your firm's relationship with a client started so long ago that no one connected with the original deal is still around. But the work keeps coming in from this loyal customer because your firm continues to do a good job. If it sounds basic, it is. This is called *repeat business*, an important reward of satisfying good customers. It is important to note that the transactional cost of signing up the next parcel of work is low under this approach because you're not formally competing for it. This offsets the high cost of capturing that client in the first place. By avoiding the need to compete, you are able to divert business development investments toward pursuing new clients, who you hope become a new generation of repeat clients. Satisfied customers frequently provide referrals to other customers, which is also a cost-effective means of attracting new assignments.

- You are selected without a competition. Award of work to your company in this manner is likely precipitated by your initiating a meeting with the client, perhaps many meetings. As you explained the qualifications of your firm and its technical experts, the client grew to appreciate your credibility. Eventually, a specific need arises, and the client asks for a proposal or price without a formal competition. After talking it over, the client decides they want to work with you. We often see this method as the province of doctors and attorneys, who rarely submit a formal written proposal to compete for work.

- You are selected for work after a formal competition. Typically, you identify or receive a solicitation (RFP or RFQ), and you respond with a written proposal. In many cases, the client then *shortlists* a subset of respondents and requests face-to-face interviews with the key team members of each firm. A formal presentation is often requested, followed by a period of questions and answers. Upon completion of the interviews, the client deliberates, scores each team, and makes a selection.

It is common for companies to achieve their sales through a combination of the methods identified above. It is important to note that there are companies who choose not to respond to RFPs. This is purely a business decision to avoid the time and cost of proposal and interview preparation. Most firms, especially those that desire to grow, must secure work in a variety of ways, and are not alone in the marketplace—they have competitors. Therefore, they must have a focused approach to connect with customers and become the preferred choice.

Getting to Know Your Customers

Classifying customers is essential to provide order to your business development program. Many business development planning efforts classify customers into the types summarized below to match successful approaches to marketing for each type. However, be careful. Never forget that customers do not label themselves. In our experience, we can almost guarantee that within a few days of the sorting process, someone within your organization will tell a client how they were classified, similar to a parent who declares which one of their children they like best.

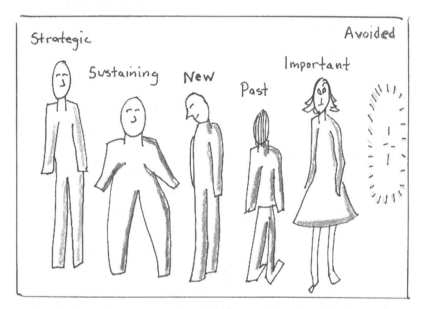

Having been forewarned, the following **table** presents an overview of the types of clients found in the portfolio of most technical professional services firms.

Client Type	Description	Marketing Approach	Commentary
Strategic	These are clients who can provide a substantial amount of work over a long period of time. Or performing work for them will help your firm achieve strategic goals.	Focus on a limited number of these, since they may require a considerable investment. Work hard to understand their buying behavior and preferences.	Typically, winning work with strategic clients is highly competitive because everyone wants them as a client. Your work for these clients will enhance your brand with other clients.
Sustaining	Clients who give you repeat business, often without a formal competition. Some firms refer to these clients as "annuity customers."	Develop and apply client service plans designed to take care of their needs. Never take them for granted. You could easily unravel many years of good service and undermine the strongest of personal relationships by ignoring sustaining clients.	Repeat business through quality work and good service will save marketing dollars for investing in other opportunities. Sustaining clients are particularly important during tough times. Periodically, a sustaining client may become a comet—in which a large project balloons revenues for several years before returning to normal.
New	A client you have not worked for in recent memory.	Sort and prioritize these clients by compatibility with your firm's strengths. Invest in educating them on your firm's differentiators.	It is difficult to sell to people who do not know you well. However, winning work with new clients is the key to revenue and profit growth, or expansion to new markets.
Past or dormant	Past client you are currently not working for.	Recognize that when the flow of work has dried up, you make a conscious decision to increase or decrease your marketing investment.	Sometimes, clients just do not have work to be performed by your firm. We often see people who continue to market these clients simply because of habit.
Important	While all clients are important, some receive more attention than others. This category provides a reminder that clients must be prioritized to maximize investments that provide the greatest results.	There is value in reviewing your list of clients through different lenses. Grouping by buying behavior is useful for planning resources, or in ensuring that the correct winning strategies are applied. Moreover, establishing priorities will help you make choices.	A firm does not want to get in a mode in which their clients are treated as if placed in a caste system. But it makes perfect business sense to have clients that you invest more time and money in than others. After all, you can't work for everyone.
Avoided	Clients for whom you choose not to do work because they do not meet your business goals, or who do not share your values.	It is crucial to review your list of clients and drop those for whom you do not want to pursue future work. It is perfectly reasonable, even advocated, to work only for clients you like. Life is too short.	We are constantly amazed by firms that work with clients who are not a fit. Firms often invest business development funds into undesired clients. We advise that avoiding a client be the one of the most careful acts your firm performs.

A firm's health can be gauged by the number and balance of clients across this spectrum. Your company should be building a business development program that actively invests time and money to attract and retain clients in the strategic, sustaining, new, and important categories, while distancing itself from the other clients. A firm's client base is not created by chance, but by choosing who it wants to work for and aligning its resources to achieve its sales goals. However, we constantly hear of people who have been working for years with clients they do not like (and vice versa) or who have no work for the firm-- all with predictable outcomes (unprofitable and inferior results).

The time and effort invested in carefully developing lists of clients, then sorting and prioritizing them will pay off in efficiency of return on investment. In many ways, this selectivity governs your destiny and is a major reason we recommend that technical professionals become involved in business development.

> *I was working with a group of people, rehearsing for an interview with a Federal client. We were sequestered in a hotel. The walls of the meeting room were covered in story-boards, which had taken over three days to prepare. We broke the presentation down into modules and were rehearsing each speaker for their portion. I was becoming frustrated with the speaker assigned to me, and he likewise with me. This was no ordinary speaker – it was a Project Manager with over thirty years of experience – someone with unquestionable credentials as a technical expert.*
>
> *As we were rehearsing, I was trying to coach him on the importance of elaborating his sales points with proofs. I was working to convince him that his claims about our wonderful experience and approach were hollow until proven. The speaker was clearly growing more upset with me, and during a heated exchange he suddenly stopped in the middle of a sentence and in an exasperating manner said, "I think you're being hyper-sensitive to the client's needs." I broke out in a grin, and said, "YES! FINALLY, YOU GET IT!"*

Why do Clients Select You?

There is no simple answer and unfortunately no complex explanation about the selection processes of clients; it's more psychology than science, and we have been studying it our entire careers. There are many published explanations of customer buying behavior. For us, as technical professionals engaged in business development, we keep it simple: <u>Clients choose</u>

service providers who they think will best meet their needs.

The real challenge is in how to understand the needs of clients, then to devise ways to best meet those needs. If this seems simple, be assured that it is not. Perhaps the best approach for making our point is to walk you through a common process for selecting a technical professional services firm. Consider a new project opportunity: one that is applying cutting-edge technology for a client who appears to be very pleasant. We can already imagine legions of young technical professionals lining up to work on this new assignment. Unfortunately, you first have to win the work. The client must choose your firm over your competitors before you are allowed to work on this plum opportunity.

This is a rude awakening for most technical newcomers. Many novices believe that their company has the best experience, the best reputation, the best technology, or even the lowest price. Even if this were true, it's rarely enough to win, a major point of this book. If being successful in business were only about technology, then anyone graduating from college with the right degree could win work. If this were true, then clearly there would be no need for professional sales and marketing people. Customers would flock to your door and line up to give you work.

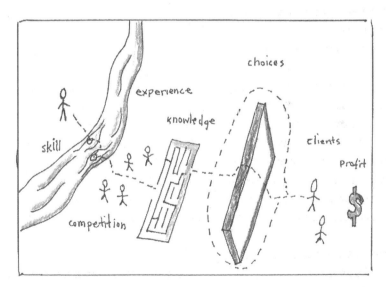

Winning new work is based on discovering a potential client who has a need which has not yet been satisfied. Sometimes, they don't know their needs. Many times, clients will not recognize a solution until they see it. Sometimes, needs are taken for granted until the fulfillment of that need is interrupted. Good examples of this include basic services, such as water supply or highway repair.

Over time, service providers learn of the client's unmet needs by engaging in discussions with them. These discussions are often helpful for the client in "thinking through" the aspects of their need. Also, as a by-product of these natural exchanges, the client learns a great deal about the advantages and disadvantages of each service provider, and begins to form opinions of who they might select for the assignment and why.

The client may award the work to whoever has provided them with the most attention or useful information. Or they may establish a competition. In some cases, the competition can be very formal and take months, or even years to reach a conclusion. Unlike today's weekend youth soccer leagues, however, there will be a winner and one or more losers. The winner will receive the assignment and reap the benefits of doing the work. The losers will move on and could face tough times until they figure out how to win. Eventually under the worst of circumstances, a firm could go out of business. Hence, the criticality of learning to be "hyper-sensitive" to client's unmet needs and developing a keen understanding of the client's reasons for selecting service providers. This is a fundamental skill that needs to be learned and improved over time.

The following table provides a brief overview summarizing common reasons clients choose one service provider over another.

Stated Reason	Implications
Superior project manager	Confidence in your leader provides comfort in his/her ability to manage project risks. This often is the easiest differentiator for the client. "We want to work with that person right there."
Superior technology	Your firm has something no one else does. Enjoy the temporary advantage before it's copied.
Solid approach	Your method for problem-solving is more workable. The process is sometimes as important as the results, and you clearly explained how you would do the work.
Lower cost	You have a lower cost of delivery. Again, enjoy it while your competition works hard to lower their costs.
Better value	Your ideas or approach were the best, saving money in the long-run, perhaps justifying the client spending more on your services than your competitor in the short-term.
Faster schedule	Time is money, and meeting schedule is often more important than superior technology.
Better communication	Free from jargon, your points were well-received and connected with the client's unmet needs. Messages were memorable and easy to understand.
Longstanding relationship	Past successful experiences working together provides comfort. You are trusted more than the competition, therefore a low-risk selection.

In our experience, clients cite combinations of these reasons for selecting one company over another. The culmination of a successful sales process is achieved by the systematic application of proven sales points based on a thoughtful competitive strategy that brings together an understanding of a client's unmet needs with a matching story of how those needs will be met, underpinned by compelling proofs, and packaged as easy to follow messages. This is complicated by the fact that clients are human and their choices are often made by a consensus of individuals who all have their own unique personalities and preferences. A winning competitive strategy needs to resonate with more than one individual, without "cancelling out" the support of another individual. Chess in three dimensions!

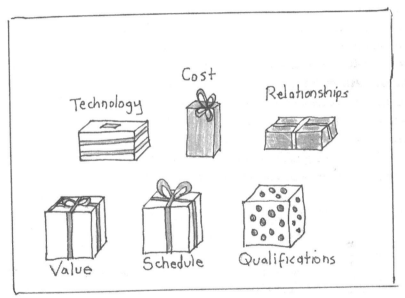

If by now you're frustrated, and have reached the conclusion that the sales and marketing process is sometimes imprecise and defies logic, then "Welcome to our World!" The profession of dealing with the uncertainty of human buying behavior is what makes it exciting. As markets and clients mature, and as competitors "pick up their game," the sales process becomes more complex. The good old days of sealing a deal over a handshake and a martini lunch are long gone. The art of understanding how to craft a winning strategy founded in the rocket science of your education and vocation is what this book is all about.

The winners leave with a prize. The losers walk away empty-handed, with only the benefit of learning from their mistakes. By understanding people's unmet needs, and using your power of persuasion, you can successfully capture a spectrum of clients.

Slowly, I gained an appreciation for how the firm made money. Clearly, technology was important as a core reason for our being hired by clients. But technology seemed to be more of a common denominator between our firm and our competitors. Of course, some firms had performed larger projects or had developed more exotic solutions. This led to their having a natural advantage at times. But we learned ways to counteract those advantages with other ideas that appealed to clients.

I'll never forget some of these early competitions, especially those we lost. I remember thinking that the news was worse than any test I had ever failed in school.

Chapter 3
The Money Side of Business Development

"Follow the money."
- Deep Throat, from All the President's Men[4]

Business Development costs were out of control. Over the years, a culture had evolved of weak accountability and lack of interest in budgeting, monitoring and controlling BD expenses. By mid-fiscal year, we were already 20% over budget for marketing and sales: a million dollars, and heading for two million by the end of the year. For larger firms this might not seem like a lot of money, but for us it was real and frightening. The worst of it was that no one felt anything could be done. We threw up our hands and resigned ourselves to tossing away millions of dollars of profit. This was money which could have been used for expansion, new services, or bonuses awarded to hard-working staff. While leadership of the firm knew that something needed to be done, they were also rightfully concerned about imposing overly intrusive rules and bureaucracy in the interest of accountability, which could potentially ruin the collegial nature of the firm. What to do?

A Business Developer's marching orders are to go forth and win new work. Accomplishing the sales goals of a technical services firm takes perseverance, talent, hard work, vision, skills, and more than a little luck. It also takes money. Most business development programs have similar missions: to achieve maximum sales with minimal cost. But where is the sweet spot between being so frugal that your efforts are compromised, or spending all your profits on winning your next sale?

The topic of money adds a third dimension to the tension between the art of selling and the technical complexity of rocket science. Profes-

---

[4] *All the President's Men*. William Goldman, Carl Bernstein, Bob Woodward. 1976.

sionals who cling to the belief that technology or "getting to the right answer" is more important than meeting a budget or making a profit will never be successful. However, we have learned that technical staff can be persuaded by the factual nature of numbers and also can be persuaded that the money side of the business helps to bring control and discipline to business development.

Financial Fundamentals

The economic drivers of the technical services industry ranges from an agreement for a few hours of consulting to contracts for the design, build, finance, maintenance, and ownership of enormous facilities. Similarly, the procurement of contracts for technical services varies widely. The services of engineers and architects are most often procured through a selection process, because they are associated with the construction industry. For those service providers that work for governmental agencies, the procurement process can in-

The natural instinct for business developers is, "Cost be damned; we need to win the contract." But then you reach a level in your career in which it becomes your job to monitor, manage, control, and squeeze usefulness from every penny of investment your firm makes. You also understand that every dollar NOT spent is a dollar added to the bottom line, of which you hopefully share a greater part.

It's an eye opener to learn the importance of prudent spending and to develop a strong compass for guiding decisions. For non-technical marketing staff, it is imperative to always remember that we are an indirect cost to our companies. As overhead, we walk a fine line between being imperative to the success of the firm and being a costly burden. In our opinion, that's actually a great place to be; it provides clarity in our careers, and in our daily decision-making. It forces us to constantly ask ourselves, "Am I providing financial value to the company today? Am I in the food chain - that direct connection between the people who need service and the people on your firm who provide service?" And when we say "between" we mean a valuable link, rather than a hurdle. That constant reminder of measuring your financial value is one of the more exhilarating aspects of the sales profession.

volve a long and expensive process of prequalifying, then bidding, then interviewing in front of selection committees in the interest of "fairness." It is not uncommon for the process of winning a single contract to cost millions of dollars and take years of effort (witness the major battles by large defense contractors for military airplanes-- in our opinion, the pinnacle of competitive sales programs).

And while time often equals money on the profit side, time also equals money on the cost side. Because of the elevated labor cost for technically-educated staff, it doesn't take long for a business development program to spend all the potential profit of a project just trying to win it.

Your company makes a significant investment in you, in a variety of ways. Let's take a look at the value of that investment, and how a marketer, and a company, can direct that investment most effectively. First, there's your salary. Assuming you have used your sales skills to negotiate a decent wage, you're likely making more than the average member of the American work-force (never forget that).

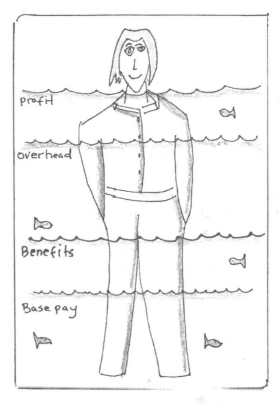

In addition to your salary, your benefits are a cost to the company. On top of that, add the tools you are provided to perform your job: (e.g., computer, software, office, cell phone, copiers, which comprise the operating overhead of your firm). In round numbers, with direct salary, benefits, and overhead, your cost can be as high as 2-3 times your salary. Of course, let us clarify that these are round numbers intended to provide a sense of the percentages. Firms and geographies vary widely on overhead, benefits, and salary.

Next, your company needs to make a profit, an important concept. Many young workers arrive on the job with opinions that the purpose of a firm is to employ as many people as possible, thereby distributing as much wealth as possible. Isn't the goal of any civilized society to improve the quality of life of its people? Certainly true, but the ability to improve people's lives by providing them an income is contingent on a company's continuing ability to sustain itself in perpetuity. And for a company to sustain itself, it needs to grow and invest in itself, using its profits, or it will stagnate, lag behind its competitors, and eventually falter and fail.

Profit can be defined in many ways, but in its simplest definition, it is the money that's left over after every expense has been paid. It is the return on the investment made by the company's owners. Your company uses this money to invest in new offices, grow into new markets, reward employees and stockholders, stave off bad economic times, and fund the dreams of its future. Without profit, most companies would not be able to be competitive with its peers for very long.

So, in addition to the costs you incur as an employee, your company would like to make a fair profit. So, it would seem reasonable for the firm to expect a return equivalent to the total costs and expected profits from your employment.

But wait a minute. The above calculations would be correct if EVERY staff member of a firm could produce sales. And you cannot presume that every employee of a company can participate in sales. (We suggest, though, that it is a useful philosophy for all employees, from receptionists to graphic designers, to ask themselves how they can best support the firm's sales effort). Compare the organiza-

> *Your company's strategy for success is to pay you what they think you're worth. Your worth is based on how well you convince them of your value during negotiations for your position or for subsequent raises. Your company also realizes that, in a free market, they need to pay competitive salaries in order to keep the best employees. That's a great metric to keep in mind, "Are you considered among the "best?" Figure out how your company defines best, then determine how you are perceived and attain or maintain that position within your firm. Again, there's clarity in how marketing and business development staff measure their value that many administrative staff or technical staff cannot attain. There's comfort in that.*

tion to one whose mission is to land an army on a beach. You wouldn't assign every person in your army to the infantry division, then load them all into landing craft and land them all on the beach at the same time. For every infantry member, there are numerous support people, everyone from cooks to mechanics to crews on the landing crafts and pilots flying above. It takes a team; some members are customer-facing, some are not.

A company is similarly organized. A word processor, drafter, or accountant would not be expected to contribute directly to sales. They are performing the important tasks of creating the work product of the company or are supporting the sales team's ability to function. So, the sales team needs to win enough new work to pay for people who cannot directly contribute to the sales effort. Consider that marketers and business developers, on average, should be focused on winning considerably more in revenue to cover more than their own cost.

> *Another question every marketer and business developer should ask is, "Am I in the middle of pursuits that will bring in revenue to the company that it would not otherwise obtain without my effort, skill, experience, or influence?"*

Therefore, every marketer and business developer needs to remember that they have the burden, as well as the opportunity, to be on the leading edge of an organization that supplies the sales needed to support those other staff members who don't contribute directly. That's a great motivator.

It's important for a firm to provide their marketing, sales, and support staff with the financial goals that the company wants to achieve. With an army, clear objectives are provided at the division level, company level, platoon level, and down to every soldier. Success is a result of providing individual objectives, while also explaining how those objectives fit with the overall goal.

Setting Investment Budgets for Business Development

Every firm has a sales goal it wishes to achieve. The dilemma is how much investment is needed to achieve that sales goal? Investing too little will mean that your competition will have more face time with your clients, will develop better proposals, and will speak at more technical conferences. Spending too much money on business development, however, means squandering potential profit and exhausting your staff on too many pursuits.

A firm should target business development spending as a percentage of the sales it hopes to achieve; the more it wishes to make, the more it might want to invest. There are published benchmarks for different types of firms which are helpful for reality-checking your sales budget relative to others. Remembering that the firm's mission is to maximize its sales and minimize its costs, targeting that sweet spot level of investment is a matter of experienced forecasting, monitoring, managing, and refining the effectiveness of your sales program—a career-long endeavor.

Directing Investments

Let's assume that a business development budget of 5% of sales is the sweet spot for your firm. The next question is, what should you spend it on? This is important and can be viewed from a few perspectives. One philosophical viewpoint is to understand that budgeting is fundamentally an act of directing investments into selected markets, clients, and opportunities, and toward achieving a company's long-term strategic plan. It's not an accounting activity, but rather an act of management from which nearly all goals can be achieved. If every activity was funded equally, then nothing would be a priority for the company, no goal more important than another.

Investing in business development involves the funding of a large number of activities to be performed by a group of people. These can range from:

- Writing competitive or sole-source proposals to clients (direct sales)
- Attending conferences or trade shows for the purpose of interacting with potential clients (indirect sales)
- Taking an existing or potential new client to dinner or other social event (a non-labor expense)
- Creating a new logo for your company brochures (communication)
- Developing a business development plan for a new technical service, or supervising the activities of the business development staff (management)
- Opening an office in a new location (strategic investment)
- Funding a large pursuit that could be a "game changer" for your firm, if won (directed investment)

These are some of the general categories into which most activities can be placed. Let's view them in more detail.

- Direct Sales. Since the primary business model of a technical services firm is to sell the talent and time of its people, then it seems obvious that potential clients would want to meet these people. Ever bought a car sight-unseen? We believe a substantial proportion of a sales budget should be invested in face-to-face contact with potential clients, listening to their needs and convincing them that your knowledge is valuable. The better a client knows you, the more they may trust your ability to care for their money. Every other activity should take a back seat to direct sales efforts. This category includes all procurement efforts, including proposals and interviews for potential clients.

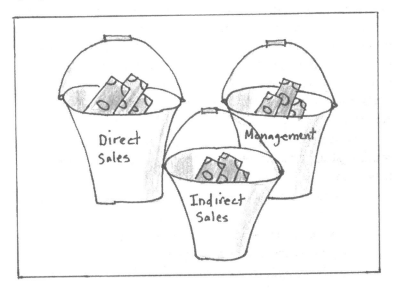

- Indirect Sales. These are the necessary investments in laying a foundation for your technical staff to more easily perform direct sales. Indirect sales activities make the prospect of meeting new clients seem less daunting to technical professionals. Imagine your top specialist arrives at a potential client's door. She/he knocks; the client answers and says, "Who are you?" That's a "cold call," the last situation in which you would want to place an uncomfortable technical expert.

Take the same scenario: your expert knocks on a client's door; the client says, "Aren't you Sarah, the person whose presentation about energy efficiency I heard at a conference? I recognize your picture from the back of the brochure I received in the mail. Come in, I have a couple questions I'd like to ask."

There is no better situation to put your technical expert in than to be asked to talk about their area of expertise in a one-on-one meeting with a client who has a need for that expertise. Indirect sales activities facilitate these types of opportunities. These "foundational" activities include developing mailings, statements of qualifications, attendance at conferences, and other work that leads your technical people to the doorstep of potential clients with the confidence of knowing they will be greeted warmly.

A problem can occur when the ratio of direct sales time to indirect sales time becomes unbalanced. Staff members often make a presentation at a conference, yet don't follow up with people in the audience. They send brochures to people, yet never knock on their doors. Managers of your business development program should be focused on assuring that a majority of your sales efforts are directed toward client contact. The budgeting process is one way to provide a metric to monitor the "balance" of activity.

- Communication. Branding and imaging of your firm (discussed in a later Chapter) often involves significant expense. Labor and expenses for items such as newsletters, announcements, and other messaging would be included here, as would maintenance and update of a web site. Some firms also advertise in professional journals, trade magazines, or other locations with high visibility to clients.

- Management. It's important to clearly separate "performing" sales from "talking about" sales, as different activities, even at the budget level. Talking about clients at an internal marketing meeting is not sales. It's an important activity, but it needs to be placed in context with the main focus of interacting with people other than your own employees.

- Strategic or Directed Investments. We also like the idea of setting up a separate category for strategic or directed investments. In some firms, this is considered to be "corporate" money toward top priority initiatives, some of which are related to business development. We've seen this budget created for winning large or strategic pursuits, which could be described as "game-changers" for the firm. In some cases, this is for directed marketing of very large clients, or technical services offered by the firm which may be in high demand. Control of this bucket of money ensures implementation of broad strategic direction from a high level. If these funds were to be distributed among the other categories, they may be well applied, and the firm could be successful, but not in a way that allows a firm to muster "overwhelming force" by concentrating its efforts. We also find that directed investments are often accompanied by specific assignment of key individuals to suspend their routine responsibilities in favor of focusing on a special program.

Directed investments may also be funds for major strategic moves, such as an acquisition, or for research and development. For some firms, this may include technical advancement of a process, or a new method of conducting work. Sometimes, these types of investments are subject to accounting and tax rules, which force them into other overhead or investment accounts. A separate identification of these funds helps to prevent their being overlooked during the process of planning new technical offerings. Similarly, acquisition of a firm, or formation of a strategic alliance to promote expansion, could fall under this category.

- <u>Non-Labor Expenses within categories</u>. There are more business development costs than simply the time charged by your people. Operating a marketing program will also include a fair amount of travel, for example. In addition, lodging and meals must be accounted for. Expenses can also include almost anything that you write a check for, such as contributions to charities.

So, once the categories are set, how do you divide your total BD budget among them? Maintaining a philosophy of investing the majority of the funds in direct sales, then distributing the rest according to the value of the category, we suggest the following percentages:

Category	Percentage of business development budget	Sub-Categories
Direct Sales	85%	Targeted Clients Prospecting for New Clients
Indirect Sales	10%	Corporate Communications
Management	5%	Strategic Planning Internal Meetings

Labor cost represents the lion's share of a business development budget. Therefore, your most precious commodity is time. Many companies budget in dollars as seen above, and begin to scrutinize expenses, while ignoring the hours invested in business development by every staff member in the firm. This is a good example of focusing on the wrong thing.

Many firms approach business development budgeting by simply accounting for a portion of the salaries of their staff from year to year. This process does not allow the company to prioritize activities or emphasize important initiatives, it merely divides the pot equally.

Time is money and vice versa, so a more appropriate method of communicating your sales investment is to convert your budget into the hours you select to be invested in business development, rather than the money available to spend. Take the sales budget percentages illustrated above, convert them into dollars (dependent on your total budget), then convert the dollars into hours (based on average hourly pay for your employees). This provides more meaning to the investment; it's a roadmap for providing your key sales-oriented staff with the freedom of time to develop and implement your sales plan.

So, with an approximate number of hours to invest in Direct Sales, you can distribute those hours among your business development and marketing staff. The hours, for example, could provide 10 people with funds to spend half their time on business development and provide them with two, full-time marketers. Or, those hours could be given to 50 people to spend 10 percent of their time on business development, without any marketing staff support. The decision on how to allocate those hours and with whom to entrust them are the most important decisions in the entire process.

To whom do you entrust your money? Some choices for people in the firm are obvious. These are the people who have a keen ability to balance sales and performance, as well as business and relationships. They are the people who are driven to sell. But, most likely, this is a relatively small percentage of the people in your firm. A relationship-based industry like ours should entrust budgets with those individuals responsible for, and capable of, building relationships that result in new contracts.

Since the bulk of the business development budget is invested in direct sales, the effectiveness of those people entrusted with the task must be maintained or the company will suffer. Some firms, over the course of time, as their business development programs mature, find that some of their high-performing sales staff lose sight of their goals, get tired, or find their interest waver, yet they continue to spend their business development budget at the same rate. Without rigorous monitoring of costs versus goals, a program can falter. That's the reason to revisit your budget and sales team regularly.

Budgeting in a Matrix Organization

Building a budget for a business development program can progress from simple to complex in very short order. A unified team providing one service from one location needs only a single business development goal and budget. Some technical services firms, however, deliver service in many geographic locations. To provide better management, these firms often subdivide their organization into smaller areas or regions. Your budgeting process must provide funding for the activities of the teams in each area. It is advantageous to consider them separate teams, especially if they work independently from each other. Each of these teams needs to feel they are responsible for their own destiny. Providing them with separate budgets gives them ownership, as long as management is careful not to create unhealthy internal competition between groups.

Let's say a firm has offices in four states. Does each receive a quarter of the total budget? If only it were that simple. Each group is likely a different size, with different sales goals and different market challenges. Some probably have a more established share of the market (most likely where the firm's headquarters is located). The firm's most recent geographic expansion is probably an area that is struggling to find its identity. So, how do you allocate budget to these regions in a way that each group feels is equitable?

> *We advise against having too many, or too few, business development cost accounts. On one hand, you'll want enough accounts to be able to understand where charges are accumulating. On the other hand, you don't want so many that it becomes confusing to those looking for a place to park their time or expenses.*
>
> *We also strongly recommend avoiding catch-all cost accounts, with titles such as "general" or "misc." These often become parking lots for those too busy to find the right job number. We've seen one of these accounts absorb over 10% of the entire firm's marketing budget. If you find an account accumulating this much expense, it's time to break it down into smaller, more meaningful accounts.*

We suggest budgeting for a sales goal that accounts for the challenges of the market conditions, then calculating a sales budget in the same way we earlier developed the companywide budget: 5% of the sales goal.

Many firms are located in a number of geographic areas and also provide a wide range of services in each of these areas. An engineering firm may provide highway design and utilities planning, a law firm may specialize in contracts and also in litigation. Using the same philosophy of providing "tribes" with a budget that they own, it seems prudent to "carve up" the overall business development budget to each service line team in each geographic location. As a result, your budget line items have grown exponentially. A matrix organization, in which the service lines in each geographic area are provided some level of autonomy, creates a three-dimensional budgeting challenge.

A firm that provides service in ten service lines in four locations has forty entities that require a sales goal and budget. Each of these sales budgets can be further subdivided into activities under separate categories, such as direct sales, indirect sales, and management, for example. Each of those budgets, subdivided into three categories has created a budgeting exercise of 120 "buckets" of funds. This is why a sales manager's best friends are the CFO and accounting department.

Accountability

The primary goal of budgeting for business development is to produce results. The simple act of budgeting is only one half of this equation. The other side of the budgeting equation is accountability. Once budgets are established and agreed upon, then the organization must shift to a mode of properly assigning costs, tracking, monitoring, and reporting. Reports of results are then used to evaluate performance.

As has been explained elsewhere, systems can be established for tracking, monitoring and reporting. In our experience, ensuring that labor and expenses are properly tracked is not to be taken for granted. This is not merely a tool for accountants. Cost tracking is a management tool for assuring effective and efficient use of resources by practitioners. Cost reports are discussed in our Chapter on Marketing and Sales Systems, but here we focus on how to evaluate those reports. Things you should be on the lookout for include:

- Routine monitoring should probably take place no less frequently than quarterly. Large accounts with a lot of charges should probably be reviewed at least monthly. This should occur in the late stages of major pursuits during proposal production or preparing for an interview, and where a lot of senior people are engaged. Evaluating the cost reports, and seeing who is charging their time, may surprise you, even if you're leading the pursuit.

- Rather than monitoring every cost account, we suggest adopting a time-tested approach of reporting by exception and identification of variances in actual costs vs. budget. A good way to approach this is to set a threshold for percent or dollars over budget. For example, you might want to identify the top ten cost accounts that are over budget on a dollar basis (also called variance), and at the top ten by percentage. Comparing the two lists will also help you see which ones may appear on both – those that do would receive our undivided attention for further review and corrective action.

- Budgets should be time-scaled to the current portion of the year. If you're three months into the year, then budgets should be calculated for the year-to-date value to calculate variances.

- Because expenses lag behind labor charges, chances are that labor charges will appear before non-labor costs are entered into the accounting system. Other non-labor costs submitted by invoice can lag even further. Such costs can include outside graphic arts support or aerial photographs, for example.

- Another method for tracking costs is to perform selected roll-ups and look at consolidated spending by important categories. Typically, these categories are best sorted along the organizational structure for your firm. For example, you might evaluate all cost accounts which accrue to a given geography, or by services lines. By looking at the totals for each category and comparing them to budget, you can quickly gain an understanding of areas that need attention. Other categories include the consolidated spending for any of the types of expenses presented earlier in this chapter, such as management and communication.

Accountability is comprised of detection, evaluation, and then action. If you're in a leadership position, it's not enough to simply identify cost or budget issues, and then throw up red flags. (Even if you're not in a leadership position, this isn't ok.) You need to do something. We encourage direct inquiries and conversations with whoever is in charge of the cost account. Follow-up conversations with specific individuals who are charging their time will tell you even more.

If you're trending over budget, there are many possible reasons. You may have under-budgeted the cost or the effort (or both) in the first place. If this is the case, a budget adjustment could be in order, as you evaluate what it will take to complete the assignment. Another possibility is that more people are working on the chore than needed or wanted. This could be a case of a manager who is overzealous in assigning resources, so a re-assessment of staffing is required. This may require you to make adjustments in the work being done, to live with less detail or less scope content. We find it's easy to run over budget during a large proposal, or in preparing for an important interview.

Being under budget may seem a blessing, especially compared to the alternative, but experience demonstrates that this condition has its downside. The reason that an account is tracking under budget may be simple, that nothing productive may be going on. Either folks don't know they should be doing something, or if they do know, then perhaps they're distracted by other priorities. If you're responsible for getting something done, it's not going to happen unless people invest time in it.

We recommend that every cost account be assigned to someone who will be responsible for whatever activity must be accomplished. This person should know they are responsible for the budget, be the "go-to" for questions, and act as the gatekeeper for charges. Creating a multitude of accounts for charges, and then assigning responsibility to one person (or worse yet, some unsuspecting marketing coordinator), is only slightly better than letting everyone charge to a catch-all account. Accountability at the individual level is the desired goal; someone must be in charge of managing the money.

Return on Investment (BD Ratio)

Another important metric is Business Development (BD) Ratio. This is the relationship between investment and return. You would like to know that, for every dollar you invest, you achieve more than a dollar in sales as a result. Earlier, for example, you budget 5% of your total sales goal as a reasonable amount to spend on achieving those sales, then you're saying that each dollar invested will result in twenty dollars in sales (or a 20:1 BD ratio). Many large firms are in search of those "holy grail" projects that cost very little to bring aboard and keep many people busy for a long time. These types of contracts might drive a firm's BD ratio to 60:1 or higher. But those same firms were once newly formed and unknown in the marketplace. They had to spend a significant amount of money to gain acceptance and trust from clients. They may have even started relationships using "loss leaders," performing work below cost to build a working relationship.

In reality, most firms achieve a large amount of their sales with little investment (a phone call from a long-time client who says, "I need you here, right away"). Yet the same firm may also invest $100,000 to win a $50,000 project for a new client (with the goal of doing a great job and building the type of relationship that prompts a phone call the following year from the client, saying, "I need you here, right away.") **Therefore, it's critical to make the right decision on which client to invest in, because it's often an enormous investment to get them onboard initially.**

Determining return on investment at the individual pursuit level can be distracting. We sometimes spend more than the potential profit on a project. We justify the investment with the mindset that a small job will grow into contract amendments, and a long-term relationship with the client, leading to more profit from proportionately less future investment. You should gauge the overall return on your investment (or BD ratio) at the client level, over a long period of time, and across the spectrum of your pursuits, including those that are intensive and those that "walk in the door."

The Role of Leadership in Managing Investments

It is a fact that neither technical people nor marketers are fond of watching budgets, much less creating them. Earlier in this chapter, we established the benefits of budgeting and cost tracking, including:

- Controlling costs allows you to manage profits.
- Knowing the limits of spending sets an expectation of accountability.
- You can avoid out-of-control proposals or initiatives (a few outliers can wreck your BD budget and profitability).
- Setting budgets allows you to chart the direction of your firm by directing investments.
- Activities that are no longer desired can be wound down by not funding them.

However, a major point needs to be made in setting budgets. Budgets are not meant to change behavior. More effective "change agents" must be applied to achieve desired changes in behavior. Simply issuing budgets will not change the character of how a firm achieves it sales objectives, and may be more counter-productive. Most people, technical professionals especially, will recoil at being managed by numbers.

Implementing change requires leadership. Healthy communication of new directions and the retirement of old activities must precede the roll-out of budgets. If explanations are provided which are consistent with the firm's strategy, and understanding is developed among staff, then budget decisions will be accepted more readily. As your firm grows, there will be an increasing tendency to manage by numbers because it seems easier. There is no substitute for leadership of people by people.

> *We were a million dollars over budget on our BD program! We knew the road to budget accountability would be laden with potholes, detours, and dead-ends. The first step was to calculate the numbers and create awareness (alarm) over the outcome of continuing in the same manner. In an employee-owned firm, it didn't take long for staff to realize this was money taken out of their own pockets. Once we gained widespread acceptance of the need for change, focus shifted to an interactive and inclusive process of engaging managers to identify new approaches. While it might have been faster and easier to simply dictate budgets, managing by numbers rarely works. We were looking for grass-roots support, enthusiastic implementation, and conformance.*
>
> *Through a series of challenging conversations, we moved toward a new system. Long-standing cost accounts were closed, and new ones were opened. Budgets were published for transparency, as negotiations quickly reached reasonable compromises on final numbers. Lingering concerns over traditional business development activities and investments were moderated, as the reality of inevitable budget cuts began to set in. Rather than taking a "meat axe" to conference attendance and advertising, a surgical approach put emotions at ease.*

One year later, business development is within 1% of budget, a vast improvement over the previous year's 20% overrun. We were also on track for meeting our sales goal. More importantly, there's no palace revolt, and no visible complaining about not having enough budget to accomplish goals. These are testimonials to a mission achieved in balancing sales, budgets, and profitability.

Chapter 4
Planning Your Business Development Program

"Here's something to think about: How come you never see a headline like, <u>Psychic wins lottery?</u>"
- Jay Leno, Comedian and Late Night Talk Show Host

We're frequently asked, "We just received an RFP in the mail, should we submit a proposal?" It doesn't matter whether the inquirer knows the client, the specific opportunity, or the competition. Does this question come from lousy engineers or scientists? Of course not. Some of the most successful technical professionals will immediately react to a promising RFP. Why? Because it's what they have been trained for.

A surprisingly common plan for developing new business is not to have one. If you work for a company where clients return to you on a regular basis, and if your hope for the future is to keep doing what you have always done, then Business Development boils down to taking orders. The phone rings, and the client asks you to do more work. You and your associates have as much work as you can handle, and you have no plans to add staff or new offices. If this is your mode of operating, then please stop reading this book. We're not going to be of any help.

Alternatively, perhaps you work for a firm in which you sit down annually with your associates, and plan your Business Development activities for the coming year. The plan considers your goals, combined with a list of targeted clients and opportunities, as well as a schedule of actionable assignments. You go out and meet these new clients, get acquainted, learn their needs, share your own ideas, and position for upcoming procurements. As the procurements take place, you are well-informed, and have become well-known, and as a result you win more than your share of the new work. If this is you, then please stop reading this book. You don't need us. In fact, we'd like to visit with you to gather your ideas and success stories.

More commonly, you work for a firm whose Business Development program is dominated by reactivity. You and your associates plug along working for clients that you have maintained for a long time. You do good work, you provide good service, and your price is reasonable. You also like your customers, and they genuinely like you. Periodically, a request comes from a new potential client for a proposal to perform a project. The scope of services is very similar to work you're already doing. Excitement builds at the thought of growing the business through new revenues. Even better, this new client is challenged by entirely different issues, so the technical solutions require innovation, making the opportunity even more interesting. You begin to write a proposal for the new client. In so doing, you sacrifice a little time you might have spent with your existing clients. You submit the proposal, attend an interview, and wait to be notified of success or failure. You also have no real idea when the next request may appear. Life gets tense when workload with current clients varies, and when you don't win enough of the proposals you write. If this is you, then stop reading this book and run (don't walk) to the bookstore to buy more copies for each of your colleagues.

The single greatest reason for reading this book is for you to understand how to take control of your marketing destiny by proactively planning your business development activities.

While technical professionals can be excruciatingly proactive and systematic in their methods of problem-solving, we find their approach to marketing to be puzzlingly reactive, if not left entirely to chance. In fact, there is a pervasive apprehension of the overall topic of marketing and business development among technical professionals. Many find sales distasteful, rooted somewhere in past experiences with used car salesmen. This is partnered with a sense that marketing is inexact and too reliant on messy human emotions. We contend that this book's principles and tools can bring confidence to technical professionals in effective business development.

We offer no guarantees. Business development is directly linked to human, emotional decision-making, which can never be fully predictable. But humans can be influenced, using those same emotional drivers. Many technical professionals recoil in fear at the prospect of wading outside the safety of the left side of their brain, which is the province of facts, figures, and differential equations. Fortunately, some of us actually enjoy operating with the right side of our brain, challenged by uncertainty and unpredictability. Success results from using the full range of thinking (rocket science) and emotions (art)—or the application of a strong technical approach to an inexact science. We know that this approach of combining rocket science and art will serve your basic need for winning work, while preserving your technical dignity.

Planning your business development program is the key to starting correctly. By committing to being organized, and deciding in advance how to approach clients and opportunities, you will improve the prospect of achieving your personal and professional goals. In a way, we're applying a bit of rocket science to art. Technologists, take comfort in the fact that reason and logic can and should be integral to sales and marketing. The very definition of planning signifies thoughtful, proactive engagement. This approach will fuel the engine of your company with work that is pragmatically and methodically procured.

> *What constitutes marketing planning?*
> - *Understand, appreciate, and be continually aware of the marketing life cycle.*
> - *Develop a diverse set of clients and opportunities to bring strength and stability to your operation.*
> - *Appropriately size your business development program to ensure that your targets, if won, will meet your business goals for backlog and growth.*
> - *Consider the effectiveness of business development staff members, along with appropriate responsibilities and activities.*
> - *Develop a pipeline of opportunities and separate those which fit your plans from those which do not.*
> - *Proactively pursue targeted opportunities, as opposed to reacting to unanticipated solicitations.*
> - *Follow through on marketing tasks and, especially, face-to-face client meetings.*

Marketing Life Cycle

The marketing life cycle depicts the natural progression of a sale, beginning with targeted client contact, identifying a basic need, moving through to selection of a service provider, satisfaction of the need, and subsequent identification of a new need. The most important concept to remember is that sales strategies and activities shadow each phase of the cycle. Sales of technical professional services do not occur as isolated transactions in which the customer discovers a need, then rushes out to buy support. Rather, sales take place in the overall context of a continuum of activities which change in response to the ebb and flow of the customer's needs and levels of satisfaction.

We could begin anywhere in the cycle, but for this exercise, let's start with identifying a new need with a targeted client. This unmet need could literally be for anything: a brand new facility, changes or expansion to an existing one, an organizational challenge, new software that solves a business bottleneck, or perhaps the need to raise rates in order to balance a budget. The client realizes that they lack the skills or available resources to accomplish the work within their own organization. Therefore, the client realizes he or she must retain the services of someone with specialized technical expertise.

As the client's need becomes more acute, he or she may begin discussions with potential service providers to learn more about their qualifications. Frequently, clients first talk to individuals they already know; thus the importance of relationships. Through these conversations, the client also develops a better understanding of their need. Service providers become increasingly engaged as they learn about the opportunity, and begin positioning to win the work. The length of this phase of the life cycle can range dramatically, from days to years, depending on urgency, money, or competing demands.

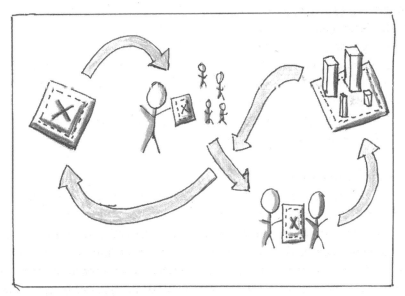

When the client feels they understand the range of potential solutions and service providers, they initiate procurement. As a simple example, he or she may send a sole-source contract to a preferred firm. If the client's policies require competition, they may invite representatives from several firms to discuss approaches to the work, how the job may be staffed, and the cost. After considering the alternatives, the client will select the firm they believe provides the best solution.

> *Procurement process from the client's point of view.*
> • **SOQ** – *Who can help me with my work?*
> • **RFP** – *Who understands my needs?*
> • **Interview** – *Who do I want to work with?*

In some cases, clients may take a more formal approach by issuing a "Request for Proposals." After receiving proposals, the client will evaluate them, then either select a firm or reduce the number of competitors to a smaller "shortlist" of the most qualified firms for further evaluation. The shortlisted firms may be invited to face-to-face presentations and interviews in front of a selection panel. Upon completion of the interviews, the selection panel convenes and makes a final decision. Contract negotiations then begin with the top-ranked firm. If negotiations are unsuccessful, then the client may terminate discussions with the firm and meet with the next highest ranked firm to consummate a deal.

Unsuccessful candidates may ask for a "debrief" to learn more about the selection panel's interpretation of the proposals and interviews. They may initiate positioning for potential future phases of the work, or for a new unmet need. Equally, some competitors may decide to forego future pursuit of new work from the client because they believe they are unable to ever meet the client's needs.

In the next phase of the cycle, the selected firm performs the work. Whatever is to be delivered, the client and service provider will meet frequently while conducting the work. Relationships are strengthened. Through a combination of performing an excellent job, and providing great service, the firm's positioning is solidified for the next potential opportunity. Such are the roots of incumbency in the marketing life cycle.

As the work is performed, the incumbent firm should be selling their services. Marketing can be most effective in this phase because the client does not feel "defensive" (as during a contracting period) and they are not compelled to adhere to strict procurement rules (because nothing official is taking place). As the project or engagement winds down, the client's attention may begin to shift to other unmet needs. During a period of incumbency, if technical professional firms take no advantage, it could lead to openings for competitors to gain the client's attention while the incumbent is focused on the current engagement and not thinking of the future.

The essence of a client-based philosophy of marketing focuses on the long-term client relationship, with sales developing regularly throughout the lifespan of the relationship. This is opposed to a project-focused philosophy, which emphasizes singular project transactions, and in which relationships often end upon completion of the assignment. Both philosophies are valid– there is no right or wrong. However, it is important to recognize the differences between the two; firms should select the path to business development which best suits the services they are able to provide.

Evaluation of Existing Clients

If you are employed by a successful company, then you already have existing clients. Guard them with your life; these customers are the bread and butter of your firm, because they already have been convinced to buy your services.

Your list of clients is the basis upon which your marketing program is built. Analysis of this list is instructive for studying the health of your program. Even small firms can have many clients. A valuable exercise is to sort your list of clients by size, such as revenue earned annually over a several year period. Focus on the top customers. Notice whether some clients are consistently on the list, year-in and year-out. These are your best customers whose loyalty transcends individual assignments. They bring you repeat business, often with decreasing amounts of effort or cost. More importantly, your lengthening relationship with these customers is likely to be increasingly more rewarding both financially and personally.

We recommend that you generate a graphic distribution of client size for your firm. If you sort your list of clients by size from smallest to largest, and accumulate the revenue of each successive client, you can plot their distribution quite easily. Reviewing this plot is instructive for several reasons. First, it is worth looking at whether your firm's portfolio of clients follows the 80-20 rule. Beginning at the right-hand side of the x-axis and working to the left, scale off the point at which you've counted 20% of your clients (by total number of clients). From that point on the x-axis, scan vertically to the intersection with the plotted line; the dollar amount between that intersecting line and the top-most point of the line (total revenue) is the amount of revenue produced by the top 20% of clients.

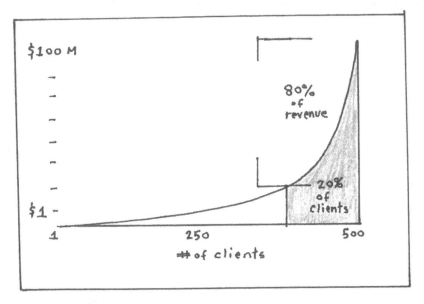

Is this analysis surprising? It is common to find out that a relatively small number of customers produce a large proportion of your revenue. Equally common is that a relatively large number of customers produce the remaining 20% of a firm's revenue. We often find this phenomenon to be even more pronounced for many firms—as much as 85%/15%. There's an old cliché about putting all of your eggs in one basket; think about what would happen to your business if just one of your top revenue producers became upset with you and cancelled your work. Conversely, it's worth thinking about how much easier it would be to generate new orders from clients who are already pleased with your performance, and are accustomed to placing large orders for service with your firm.

> *The Pareto Principle is also known as the 80-20 rule, or the law of the vital few. Simply put, it states that for surprisingly many events, roughly 80% of the effects originate in 20% of the causes. Dr. Joseph Juran suggested the principle and named it after Italian economist Vilfredo Pareto who observed in 1906 that 80% of the land in Italy was owned by 20% of the population. A common rule of thumb in many businesses is that 80% of your sales come from 20% of your clients. Our experience with technical professional services firms also validates this principle.*

This is important! One of the oldest principles in marketing is that the easiest task is to sell something you know how to do, to people you know. Those customers in the top 20% of your list have proven their buying power, and their predilection to select your firm.

- You should sell more of what you are good at, to existing customers who know you. This is the basis for selling more of the same thing you are already doing, something often ignored by engineers who are focused only on doing their job, and not the next project.

- The second major point is that if you are beginning a new service, or introducing a new technical expertise as an offering for your company, it is usually best sold to customers you already know. This is known as cross-selling, and it can work because your customers already trust you, and would be willing to take a chance with you doing something new for your firm.

- A third point is that if you're trying to add new customers, it is best to sell them something tried and true for your firm. This is because your reputation and experience are proven, and the customer who does not know you will seek comfort in the fact that you should know what you are doing.

- A trivial fourth point is that it is pretty darn hard to sell to new clients a brand new service for your company. While this may seem obvious, it is not to many engineers. It is illustrated to underscore the point that selling to old customers is the strongest strategy of all.

Moreover, the other customers on your list bear closer examination. Could you sell more to the next 20% of customers? Take a look at the percent of revenues produced by the Top 40%, and you may find that it produces 90% of the revenues of your firm. This is a target-rich environment! These people know you, and you know them, so it makes sense to continue to sell to them.

This discussion would be incomplete without some notes about the clients to the left of the median. By definition, the median is the amount of revenue produced by the client at the 50th percentile. There are a lot of very good reasons for having relatively small clients in your list, and one very bad one– chance. We could write an entire book about the strategies of companies looking only to work with large clients. Inevitably, these strategies result in forcing out small clients. Sometimes, this is the right thing to do, especially for a large company. Small clients can take up time from key personnel that are better directed to larger clients. They can also result in a cost of sales that is proportionately much higher than the cost for large clients.

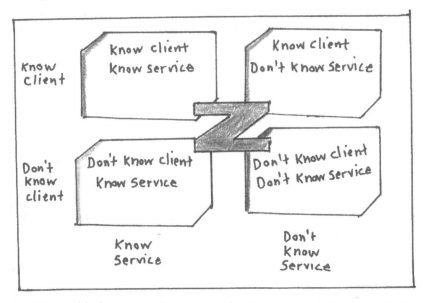

We could also argue the merits of selling to small clients, including the prospect of their growing to become large clients. Small clients tend to be more user-friendly (although not always) and therefore are less demanding and less risky. A small client can be a good "training ground" for junior staff.

It is also important to keep in mind that your analysis of revenues may also identify relatively smaller *revenue producers* who may in fact be large clients for your competitors. This may be because your firm has not figured out how to earn a larger share of a given client's business. If this is the case, then smaller contracts can be a good way for a firm to prove itself to a large client. This is a recognized strategy for penetrating a new client: positioning for larger opportunities by building relationships and expanding your knowledge of the client.

An illuminating way of further analyzing this topic is to simultaneously rank the amount of business development expenses you incur by client, compared with their revenue. If you do not have an accounting system which can do this, then you need one. By organizing your cost-accounting system to capture this information, and training staff to code their timesheets and expenses appropriately, a great deal of strategic information can be mined. Our question is, "would you find your firm investing the majority of its marketing budget in the 20% of clients which provide 80% of the revenue?" We'd be surprised. Rarely do firms consciously allocate their marketing budget by client this proactively. However, if you are spending a disproportionately large share of your marketing budget on the smallest revenue producing clients, then you should be asking, "What is wrong with this picture?"

Identifying New Clients

While you may have a terrific stable of existing clients, all businesses need new clients. The process of identifying new customers, and convincing them to select you for work, is one of the greatest challenges in business. Referring back to the points made previously, the toughest thing to do in marketing is to sell to people you do not know, even if you're in command of the technical content. There are a number of means of identifying new clients:

- Professional clubs or industry associations. Explore the organizations where customers gather for common interests. The membership list for these organizations is often tailor-made for identifying new clients. Many companies organize their business development efforts around these associations.
- Technical journals. Publications are often issued by the industry associations discussed above. Look for authors who work for potential clients. Alternatively, seek articles dealing with technologies that fit your skills, and identify examples where they are practiced on potential clients. Online search services can scan vast media resources for key words, then forward relevant articles to your e-mail.
- Personal relationships. Someone you know may have changed jobs. Keep track of friends and acquaintances through your networks.
- Word of mouth. One of the oldest methods of identifying new business opportunities, which still works today, is through referral. Talk to your current clients about others with whom they associate. If you are having a good experience working for a client, you may find success working for their colleagues.

- Vendors and suppliers. It is common for suppliers to call on your technical staff with an interest in getting their products specified. Many of these same sales people also call on customers who may be potential clients for your firm. As a result, they often hear of upcoming opportunities, which they may readily share with you. Subconsultants and teaming partners may also share in your search for new clients.
- Competitors. Hopefully you know who your competitors are. Informal discussions with them often lead to work they're doing for their clients. These discussions can offer a wealth of information on prospective customers who are dissatisfied with your competition.
- RFPs. Solicitations often arrive from customers for whom you are not working. And of course, RFPs are often advertised in the journals of commerce. We don't recommend that you blindly respond to them. However, unanticipated RFPs can offer insights about these clients. Just because you do not intend to pursue an RFP, doesn't mean you shouldn't read it and learn about their selection process and their unmet needs.

Developing a Sales Pipeline of Project Opportunities

In addition to developing a list of current and potential new clients, an important part of marketing planning is to compile a list of project opportunities for them; this list is often referred to as a sales funnel or pipeline.

There are good reasons to keep a list of leads; the most important of which is so you don't forget them. It's easy to get caught up in day-to-day business, or be pulled in the direction of bright shiny objects, losing track of long-term, strategic pursuits.

There are many valid ways of structuring your sales pipeline, but as a minimum you'll want to track:

- Existing vs. Targeted Clients. As stated above, it is important to prioritize opportunities where you're selling to existing customers separately from targeted new clients.
- Leads and Opportunities. Opportunities should include all competitive and sole-source leads, contract renewals, and potential amendments. By including all leads (rather than only ones that are competitive), the sales pipeline becomes an accurate predictor

not only of sales, but also of future revenue. The pipeline can serve as one of the best forward predictors of financial performance available to your firm. Your CEO will bow to you for providing such a valuable tool.

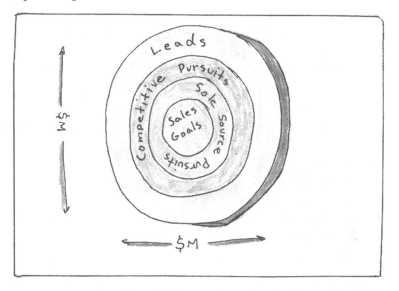

- <u>Timing</u>. You should track the anticipated arrival date of an RFP, as well as predicted start date of the project. This information allows you to plan the deployment of marketing and technical resources. We often hear that it is impossible to know the timing of procurements with certainty. We recognize this and understand that procurements are often delayed. Do not accept these arguments as reasons for not adopting a sales pipeline. Despite these points, we assert that you should "do your best" with the information available.
- <u>Revenue potential</u>. You should attempt to estimate the potential income your firm may earn from each opportunity. Again, many individuals resist this because of uncertainty, but an educated guess is better than nothing at all. In addition, if you do not even know the value of an opportunity, are you really having an effective conversation with the client? Knowing the timing of future revenue will allow you to reality-check future sales goals and BD budgets.

- Probability of success. For each opportunity, you should provide a conservative, but realistic, assessment of the percentage probability of being selected. We recommend that you don't get too scientific here. We've witnessed debates over whether the probability of a win is 55% or 65%; this degree of precision is within the "noise level" of the estimate. A suggested range could be: 25% where there is competition, 75% where you are the front-runner, and 90% where it is sole-source but not a "sure thing." Note that a significant mission of business development is to drive your chances of selection upward from 25% (openly competed) to 75% (front-runner) during the life of a procurement. By multiplying the percentage of selection against estimated contract value, you can produce a forecast of future sales. We often refer to these as "factored fees," because they are dependent on your assessment of both value and prospect of success.
- Start Date. A continuous flow of revenue to run your firm means that you need a continuous stream of sales. A healthy portfolio of leads should be tracked that provides this stream of opportunities.
- Sorting characteristics. Other designations will allow you to sort your pipeline into pertinent groupings. For example, many businesses offer more than one type of service. By identifying the nature of each lead, you'll be able to evaluate discrete portions of the sales pipeline. Examples include geography, type of service, client manager, or other subdivisions.

Many firms adopt simple tools, such as a spreadsheet, for beginning a sales pipeline. As firms grow, or more complexity is desired, more powerful software, such as a relational database, can be adopted.

Generating New Leads

Tracking leads is important, but first they must be identified. There are numerous sources, but the best source of leads is directly from the horse's mouth. This is why face-to-face client contact is the most productive marketing activity.

When conversing with existing clients, many technical professionals are so engaged in their current work that they forget to ask about future opportunities. You can solve this problem by asking your client managers to focus on tomorrow's opportunities, while the project team focuses on today's work. Other sources of generating new leads are in the same places one locates new clients, including:

- <u>Networking</u>. Other clients, vendors or service providers can be a source of information about leads because they circulate with the same customers.
- <u>Databases or published lists</u>. If your business is driven by regulatory compliance, quite often lists are published of agencies or companies who fail to meet required standards. Also, local and regional business journals publish lists, often ranked in order of size, for firms doing business in a particular industry.
- <u>News</u>. Believe it or not, reading the local newspapers can provide quality information on upcoming opportunities. Many agencies or companies appear in the news. We like the free automated clipping services now available which search many online news services based on keywords, and then deliver the results to your e-mail.
- <u>Internet</u>. Increasingly, clients advertise their procurements online. Notifications are often received by subscribing to them at a web site. The largest potential client of all, the United States Government, advertises online through CBD-Net or www.fedbizopps.gov.
- <u>Lead services</u>. There are companies that review numerous sources, then consolidate leads by category or key words. These services provide solid information, but these notifications are typically sent to fifty of your favorite competitors, as well.

Once a client announces a desire to hire a technical professional, an opportunity is born. Information about opportunities should be protected because of their immense value to your company.

It is essential to subject leads to a qualifying process. We liken the task to a real estate agent qualifying potential home buyers. One of the first questions asked by an agent is how much income you make. That information allows them to readily determine the mortgage you can afford. They will wisely show you only those homes which you can afford. Leads for technical services must be qualified in a similar manner. There's no sense pursuing opportunities that you can't win. However, leads have more possible angles than mortgages. For example:

- Is the lead realistically within the capabilities of your firm? Has your staff successfully performed similar projects in the past, or would it be a stretch?

- Do you have the resources to complete the work within the contemplated schedule? If not, can you team with another firm or identify resources which can be secured to get the work done?
- How widely known is the lead? If it was obtained from a newspaper article or lead service, then you can assume that the "world" knows. If there are many competitors, will your firm stand a realistic chance of winning?
- Timing is everything – will the RFP be released any day now, or will the lead allow you 6-12 months to prepare for the selection process? If you have time, then will your firm be able to pull together a winning strategy and commit to positioning activities?

Consideration of these and other factors should form the basis of whether a lead is added to your company's marketing pipeline and becomes formally targeted as a pursuit.

It is important to keep in mind that market conditions can be quite dynamic; economies can take dramatic turns, upward or downward. We recommend that sales pipelines be revisited often.

Selection of Targeted Pursuits

Perhaps the most important decisions made in your marketing program are in selecting targeted pursuits. Rather than allowing pursuits to select you (reactive approach), you designate those opportunities in which you will invest time and money for positioning, proposals, interviews and winning (proactive approach). This is consistent with our overarching theme of taking command of your marketing destiny.

If you're fortunate, selecting and prioritizing targeted pursuits will be an exercise in making tough choices from a rich pipeline of attractive leads. A systematic approach to decision-making helps make these choices. Many firms develop a simple set of criteria for scoring opportunities, which further refine the "probability of success." You could include:

- **Get**– this evaluates the probability of winning an opportunity, based on an evaluation of criteria, such as knowledge of the opportunity, strength of client relationship, technology fit, and suitability for your strategic goals.
- **Go**– this is a further determination of whether an opportunity should become a pursuit. If your "get" rating is high, then the opportunity is likely a no-brainer to "go."

These criteria allow you to *compare* opportunities against one another and help in making *choices*. As we stated earlier, the objective of positioning is to move an opportunity from a low win probability to a higher one, from being one of the pack to the front-runner. Note that the "Get" assessment is conducted early in your awareness of the opportunity, and should be updated periodically in your pursuit process, to continually reinforce your commitment. If the nature of the opportunity changes, such as the entrance of a powerful competitor or an unexpected staffing change, then you might shift your focus to better opportunities.

When realistically considering pursuits, you must be prepared to adjust your priorities. It is within your control to adjust the priorities of your staff, the amount of their available time, and their assignments. **These are powerful gears in your business development machine, if you regulate them skillfully.** We recommend that sales pipelines be revisited periodically, at least every six months. Marketing leadership should update the pipeline continuously, as new leads are identified or discarded.

> Many clients award sole source contracts to consultants who develop projects. In one case, for a major international program management assignment, the consultant who spawned the project objected, and rightly so. They asserted that a sole source award of such a large contract would either be protested, or create such misgivings that the consultant's effectiveness would be severely weakened.
>
> In response, the client held a competition, and the firm which created the idea was successful. All those meetings and interaction between the consultant and the client in fleshing out the program management approach to the client's problems formed solid relationships which contributed to the successful win.

Creating New Opportunities

Many firms are successful pursuing projects conceived by their clients. However, some firms take their game to the next level by **creating** the opportunities that they pursue. This is one of the highest forms of business development, because it involves developing solutions to problems for your clients before they realize a problem exists. Isn't this what clients most want from technical professionals? Consider the following strategies when contemplating how to develop proactive solutions for clients:

- You will have a better chance of success with clients who already trust you, but we have seen this work well with new clients, too.
- Develop a culture in your business development program in which you often convene for brainstorming sessions. Discuss unconventional solutions; move out of the rut of bringing old, but safe, ideas to the client. While many of the outside of the box ideas won't work, there's a good chance that one or two might have merit, if tweaked.
- Bring your ideas in the form of choices. Don't be too defensive—the intent is to work with your client. Once you've explored ideas together, then sit back and listen. Watching your client weigh the pros and cons of ideas may be the single greatest benefit of the entire process, even if they don't adopt any of them.
- The client will appreciate your sincerity in proactively thinking about their problems. This is a sure relationship-builder.

Some may think that a client will take your hard work and shop it to your competition. This is a measured risk almost always worth taking. If the client competes the opportunity, your firm should be a front-runner, because of the high quality nature of your meetings with the client and the development of relationships in the process. Moreover, creating your own opportunities is less expensive than the cost of chasing opportunities that were created by your competitors.

Planning for Diversity of Clients and Projects

Actively planning for a range of types of customers and projects can successfully insulate your practice from market swings. Although it might be tempting to develop business by focusing on a core business or service line, diversity brings stability and strength. By compiling, comparing, and contrasting the characteristics of clients and projects, you can actively plan for diversity.

In many firms, revenue potential tends to override the thought process for selecting who and what to pursue, because dollar-size is an easy metric to evaluate. However, there are other important lenses to use as a filter when reviewing your stable of clients and pipeline of opportunities.

Existing vs. New Clients

Of all the dimensions of diversity, comparing existing and new clients is the most revealing. It is almost always more costly to win work from a new client than from an existing client. A program too far weighted toward existing clients risks losing its edge in competing against other firms for new clients. (Keep in mind that winning work from existing clients can be competitive or sole-source.) In contrast, it is not uncommon for existing clients to be overlooked as business development activities focus more toward the hunt for new clients.

The question becomes one of how to achieve balance in directing time, resources, and energy to both groups of clients. We contend that somewhere between a quarter and a third of your pursuits should be for new clients, with the rest dedicated to existing clients. Many factors can influence this; for example, if you were in the midst of several large, multi-year assignments with existing clients, and had marketing budget "to spare," then you might invest more in expansion of your business with new clients, anticipating the end of the large programs.

Profitability

Are you aware of how profitability is derived from clients? If your accounting system allows you to determine profitability by client, then you may wish to conduct an analysis. You may find that your largest revenue producing clients do not generate profits on a higher percentage basis at the same rate as other clients. And you should not be surprised if the profits from some of your largest or longest-standing clients are not very attractive. Over time, there is a tendency for erosion of profitability, resulting from successively tougher contract negotiations. Profitability is a key factor for prioritizing a client or pursuit.

Perhaps an even more important measurement is the return on investment (ROI) afforded by each of your clients. ROI considers not only the contract's profitability, but also incorporates marketing and transactional costs (such as the aging of receivables). As a result, what appears to be a healthy profit can be greatly reduced if the client takes a long time to pay its bill, and you're forced to borrow money to cover salaries until the check arrives.

Also, we find that many people believe that marketing costs are zero for clients who provide "repeat business" with no formal proposals. However, experience demonstrates that costs for scope development, for example, can grow to become quite substantial, and should be monitored.

Types of Service

The vast majority of technical professional services firms provide more than one type of service. Even small firms can easily find themselves offering over a hundred separate services to their clientele. By categorizing clients and pursuits according to types of service, you may gain an appreciation for the diversity of your marketing targets across a different dimension. You can determine if you are tracking enough of a given service to keep the specialists busy within that area of expertise.

In addition, you can readily determine if a market is declining or growing— an insight upon which you can make strategic decisions. A declining market, based on a decreasing level of leads, would suggest you should downsize or cross-train specialists to a more productive service. An increasing market would prompt you to recruit new talent.

Our Corporate strategic plan called for developing design-build as a new delivery method for projects. The new service would help clients by combining engineering and construction into a single service, making our firm a "one-stop shop" for results. For us, it offered increased revenue and profitability from larger, more complex projects.

Our local office was excited with the prospect of a major new extension of services. We made plans to emphasize design-build on several opportunities that were targeted in the upcoming year. Additionally, we committed to create new projects by convincing clients to convert traditional contracts to this new alternative. We prepared to make a major thrust. And it almost collapsed the office.

Amidst the enthusiasm of the new strategy, no one considered the prospect that every pursuit could be lost. Also, because of the much higher cost of each design-build pursuit, there were far fewer proposals that year. All of our eggs were in the design-build basket. There was precious little diversity in the nature and type of services pursued. The outcome was decreased sales, a drop in revenues, and ultimately staff reductions.

As you evaluate the diversity of your marketing opportunities with respect to types of services, keep in mind the natural progression of many assignments. If your market outlook suggests that a number of clients are currently conducting planning studies, then it would be reasonable to predict that implementation of those plans will be upcoming. In the engineering arena, clients in the midst of designing new facilities will likely require construction management services in the near future. A single lead may bear fruit several times during its life-cycle.

Geography

Sorting your clients and opportunities by region, state, country, or other pertinent boundary will allow you to determine if your customer mix offers geographic diversity, and can provide a buffer from localized fluctuations in economic activity. Balance in this category can be especially challenging because it is not easy to move technical professional resources across a map. However, big picture movement of people across regions should be evaluated if the long-term outlook justifies the investment.

Strategic Direction

Assuming your company has a strategic plan, are you doing your part to achieve its goals? Hopefully, you'll take this as a friendly reminder to re-read your strategic plan and look for the new services, geographies, and technologies targeted by your leaders as a path to future growth. Determine which customers will allow you to present new offerings even though your firm lacks an extensive track record. Marketing and sales are on the leading edge of developing opportunities that help you achieve your long-term aspirations.

Balance of Probability

If you were to honestly assess your probability of winning projects across your pipeline, what if the majority of your projected sales fell below 25% chance of success? This would make us pretty nervous about the future. It would be better to have fewer opportunities, but each with a higher prospect of success. Sorting your leads by the degree of anticipated competition, you can evaluate whether a balance has been struck between "fairly sure things" and "hotly contested pursuits."

Most firms can't afford to chase pursuits that are so low in probability of success that they would require an inordinate commitment of resources, effort, and expense. By sorting your leads, you will be able to prioritize those competitive pursuits which realistically can be won, applying resources where they would be the most successful, while also achieving other diversification goals, such as high potential for profitability, wide range of services, or maximum spread across your company's geographies.

Likeability

Previously, we discussed the importance of working for clients with whom you get along. While this may seem trite, it is decidedly not. Talk to your staff and ask which clients are more enjoyable to work with. We have noted a tendency to become complacent over the years by working for the same clients. As time passes, relationships tire, and each side begins to take one another for granted. Deterioration may reach a point where no one on your staff wants to work with these clients. If this is your situation, then do these clients a big favor and decline to pursue their work. You do these clients a disservice if you continue to provide less-than-excellent work.

While some of these diversification categories may seem obvious, we've seen them routinely ignored. In firms where reactive marketing is the norm, there is no thought given to sorting and analyzing your clients and opportunities. This simple activity, combined with a modest amount of reflection, will help you achieve a successful balance in your business development approach.

Sizing Your Business Development Program

Once you have developed a list of clients, and your sales pipeline is growing with leads, it is important to assess the size of your business development program. First, consider the annual revenue of your firm, office or market sector. Then factor in any prescribed growth rate, which has been set by management. For illustration, let's assume that your current annual revenues are $9 million, and your business unit desires to grow to $10 million next year.

You need to consider a reasonable average success rate for procurements pursued by your firm. While your hit rate may vary, let's assume that you win one in three procurements on a dollar basis. However, consider separating your procurements into two categories: 1) for repeat and/or sole source business and, 2) for open, competed procurements. This is important because your success rate is different for each type. Applying an average overall success rate over both categories could lead to misleading conclusions, which may result in your marketing program being under or over planned. If we assume that your historic success rate is 90% for sole source contracts, and these constitute one-half of your sales target ($5 million), then you're only faced with competing for and winning another $5 million at a (historic average) 33% hit rate. This greatly improves the focus of your program because it translates to pursuing $15 million in sales volume, which is one-half of the amount you would have calculated using a 33% hit rate across all your leads (and underscoring the importance of repeat business).

We frequently hear of business units pursuing a sales volume roughly equal to their annual revenue goal. This approach falls short because they won't be selected for every pursuit. It always amazes us during conversations with teams of technical professionals who have not done the math on how many leads should be pursued. They do not size their marketing program when considering their win rate or growth demands. The simplest of calculations will show if you're in the process of selling enough work to achieve your goals.

The next step in sizing your marketing program is to develop a sense of the size of your overall sales pipeline. Keep in mind that the sales pipeline is the entire universe of opportunities that could be reasonably pursued, because they are within reach of your marketplace. In other words, the sales pipeline should incorporate opportunities known to your firm, which could be deemed winnable, if you were to apply good positioning efforts. Obviously, being "winnable" is subject to the weighting concept we previously introduced, but these include projects within your technical skills, experience, and geographic reach. We would include opportunities with clients where you do not necessarily have strong current relationships. If your pipeline has a horizon of 3-5 years, then you should have

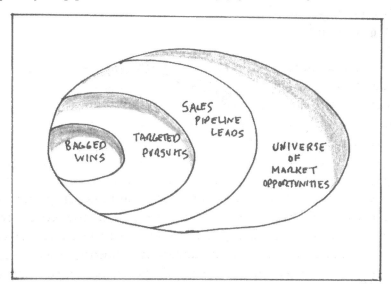

enough time to build relationships through good positioning.

While markets vary, a good rule of thumb would be to strive for a targeted sales pipeline at least three times larger than the volume of opportunities for which you will actually compete. There is clearly some art involved here, but continuing from the previous example, if your goal is to win $10 million in sales, and half of your pursuits will be competed at a 33% success rate, then your $15 million in competed pursuits ideally require you to target $45-50 million in your sales pipeline as identified leads and opportunities.

It's a judgment call, of course, but if you're tracking $50 million in bona-fide opportunities, we feel pretty confident you will generate the needed $10 million in sales ($5 million in repeat business at 90% chance, and $5 million from winning a third of $15 million in competitively pursued opportunities). If your pipeline of leads is any smaller, then you will not be able to be as selective as you wish in your pursuits, and you may not win enough work to meet your revenue goals.

Here's another wrinkle: we need to make the point that sales are not the same as revenues. Revenues represent the billings to clients for labor and other costs in conducting work. Sales, on the other hand, are the one-time bookings of new contracts that will eventually turn into revenue. The most important thing to keep in mind is that revenues are earned over a period of time, while sales represent a single event. Revenues are tied to a schedule; in some cases earned at a relatively constant rate over the life of a project. Frequently, however, revenues are earned at a sporadic rate. Consider an opportunity for which, if selected, your firm will book $1 million in sales. A very nice sale. However, what if the project schedule is three years, and the revenues are slowly earned at the beginning, then peak in the third year? This means that although you've booked a sale, it may not keep many of your staff busy in the first 12-24 months—a long time to maintain a staff. One goal of planning your marketing program, from an operations point of view should be to balance workload. This strongly suggests that you consider selecting leads in full knowledge of how the revenue will flow into the firm.

If you have enough leads in your pipeline, then your marketing program can focus on positioning and proposals. If you don't have enough opportunities, then your team should be out prospecting and generating new leads. Under the gun of deadlines, it is common for technical professionals to overlook the steps in sizing their program. By following these guidelines, you can not only achieve your strategic plan goals, but also safeguard your business against downsizing.

Assigning Business Development Time and Resources

The next step in planning your BD program is to "get feet moving in the right direction." Allocating time is important to ensure that the right resources are targeted to business development tasks. Consider first the following main categories of staff members that have varying levels of time dedicated to sales.

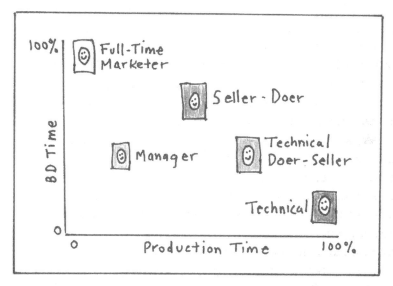

- <u>Full-time marketer</u>. These are 1) technical staff whose reputations and ability to sell work provide more value to the company than the hours they can bill to clients performing their specialty, and 2) marketing staff who dedicate their time to pursuits. They allocate 100% of their time to sales.
- <u>Manager</u>. Many middle-managers find themselves dividing their responsibilities in thirds between management, sales, and technical work. Many managers will find it difficult to set aside responsibilities in one or more categories to dedicate to major pursuits. One of leadership's more important tasks is to encourage managers to stay externally-focused as opposed to devolving into a life of signing timecards and expense reports. Also, managers must lead by example, and do what is needed, rather than doing what is comfortable.

- <u>Seller-Doer</u>. This is a category of professional who wears "many hats." They are often client service managers, and also oversee execution of assignments. These are often individuals who are comfortable talking about a wide range of technical topics to a variety of people, while retaining their technical skills in a handful of specialties. Since they perform much of the work they sell, they may only be able to dedicate a quarter of their time to sales. Sometimes a firm has difficulty winning large pursuits when the Seller-Doer doesn't have enough time to dedicate to sales.
- <u>Technical Doer-Seller</u>. Technical activities dominate the responsibilities of the Doer-Seller. Typically, they will be called upon to develop technical ideas, scopes, or estimates for proposals. In addition, they can be called upon as Subject Matter Experts to accompany Client Service Managers on visits to clients. Perhaps 10% of their time is dedicated to marketing.
- <u>No marketing time</u>. These are individuals with no budgeted marketing time, purely technical staff, or administrative staff such as accountants and receptionists.

Consider the type of people you have in your sales force, their availability, the amount to time they can dedicate to sales, and the magnitude of your sales goals to determine whether your sales force is "right-sized." If you do not have enough of the right people, with available time for business development, then you won't achieve your marketing goals. Ensure that you have a realistic balance of people and activities. Exceeding your business development capacity will result in overburdening your staff, burnout, and weak performance, which is a threat to your success.

Beginning with your firm's strategic plan, and any identified goals (e.g., for revenue, profit, sales, risk, and achieving strategic objectives), you can begin to plan the alignment of the right staff with your marketing needs. You should also consider their personal strengths and weaknesses, and willingness to participate. This staffing plan becomes the cornerstone in managing business development activities and achieving results.

Shifting our focus from individuals to overall business units or teams of professionals, we often find that organizations become unbalanced in how they spend their marketing time. A revealing question to ask your staff is how they spend their marketing time. The responses typically land in the following distribution:

- Proposal and interview preparation (50%)
- Visibility and networking (25%)
- Direct face-to-face client contact and positioning (20%)
- Post-selection negotiations (5% or less)

Such a distribution of time is indicative of a disproportionate amount of investment in proposals to make up for lack of face-to-face client contact. In many cases, these proposals are for unanticipated procurements because of infrequent client contact. Also symptomatic of this approach are client contacts at visibility events, such as conferences or professional meetings, which are important, but not as much as face-to-face meetings with clients on their turf. In our view, a stronger program distribution would be:

- Direct face-to-face client contact and positioning (50%)
- Proposal and interview preparation (25%)
- Visibility and networking (15%)
- Post-selection negotiations (10%)

This distribution emphasizes quality meetings with clients, building relationships, and developing insight on leads. Client contacts not only improve your positioning for competed procurements, they also cement your position for add-on and sole-source work. You can see that this program obviously sets aside less time (and money) for proposals, but because your client contacts have been fruitful, your odds of success are much higher when you have positioned your firm as the front-runner. Note that there is less emphasis on visibility and networking under this approach. If planned well, these activities are highly effective and can be a valuable component, particularly in attracting new clients to your firm. However, they are not substitutes for client contacts. Also note that additional time is spent in negotiations and ensuring that final scope, contract terms, and conditions are in agreement between the firm and its clients.

We find that organizations that take command of their marketing destiny actively implement their programs by emphasizing client contacts in their assignments of staff. By placing clients "first," the other elements of the marketing program should complement that decision in a balanced approach across many individuals.

Implementing Your Plan

Managing a business development program calls for oversight of everything we've discussed in this chapter. This responsibility is like conducting a symphony, bringing together many diverse activities and individuals to achieve a common goal of winning new work. Inherent in marketing program planning is achieving balance among these many activities. Throughout this book, we extol the virtues of controlling your own marketing destiny by taking the initiative, being proactive, and methodically planning your business development program.

At the weekly marketing meeting, the discussion centers on an RFP that was received that week, which had been anticipated, and which the team had actively pursued for many months. Much of the discussion also focuses on upcoming brainstorming sessions about challenges that some customers face, but may not be aware of. Capture plan sessions are scheduled, and appointments for client contacts are double-checked to ensure that team members understand their tasks.

In between marketing meetings, RFPs show up in the mail unanticipated. They aren't ignored or tossed in the trash. Rather, they are duly studied for patterns of buying by potential future clients. However, despite great temptation, no one asks the question, "Should we submit a proposal?" All is well in the world.

Chapter 5
The Competitive Value of Client Service

"Too many people think only of their own profit. But business opportunity seldom knocks on the door of self-centered people. No customer ever goes to a store merely to please the storekeeper."
-Kazuo Inamori, entrepreneur and founder of Kyocera Corp

> *Inside the conference room sat a sea of glum faces. My colleagues and I were planning for an upcoming potential opportunity with an important client. We had designed their last project a few years prior and badly wanted this new project. As we evaluated our standing with the client, it became clear the last project had not ended well. We discussed the problems and a handful of lingering issues remained from an otherwise successful job.*
>
> *First, there was a vibration problem within a pump station. Although the pumps performed as designed, the operators grew concerned that vibrations would eventually cause a failure. Second, there were problems whenever it rained. Water puddled in the parking lot, because of uneven paving. This was shoddy work by the paving subcontractor, but our construction inspector missed it. To make matters worse, a leak in the operations building roof consistently reminded the client of poor workmanship during bad weather. The meeting attendees wondered aloud if we should simply fold the tent and not propose, even though our qualifications were impeccable.*

Make no mistake, sales are critical, but good client service is what makes for a successful, long-lived business. It forms the foundation for achieving and sustaining satisfied customers. This, in turn, leads to repeat business, which is the lowest cost means of winning work.

We've discussed how most technical professionals believe that getting to the right answer constitutes a "good job." And, after performing well, they often expect the next project or assignment to be handed to them. Unfortunately, it isn't always good enough. That's because delivering a correct "technical" answer became the "expected norm" long ago. Another way of putting this is that failure to perform technically will likely lead to your not being rehired by the client. This is because the right answer is necessary, but often insufficient. **How you treat the client can frequently be as important, if not more important, than what you do.** This chapter focuses on the direct link between client service and winning more work, whether by competition or sole source. We're not talking about buying three-martini lunches or sending flowers when your firm fouls up. These tactics are trivial, along the lines of cutting your price. Instead, we deal specifically with how to approach client service when winning the

A busy regional office of a major consulting firm experienced a business downturn. Orders were issued from corporate headquarters to cut staff, and the receptionist was the first to go.

It didn't take long for clients to begin to complain openly. They liked the previous receptionist, because she connected them instantly when they called. She even recognized them by voice, and greeted them by name. Now that she was gone, when clients called, they were greeted as strangers. Clients noticed that the new temporary receptionists were harried, leading to callers being connected to the wrong extension or being dropped altogether.

Your receptionist is likely the one consistent voice your clients hear. Day in, day out, they handle phone calls, and greet clients. When they do a good job, they're almost never noticed, even taken for granted. But when a good one is suddenly gone, the feedback can be surprising.

The next time staff reductions are contemplated, think twice before letting go of the receptionist. In fact, such an important person in your overall client service strategy should probably be rewarded, rather than being the least paid person under your roof (see our chapter on Branding).

next assignment is on the line. Achieving high levels of client service is a valuable differentiator.

We find that of all the aspects of business development which puzzle technical professionals, this topic is at the top of the list. All of the education, training, experience, and hard-wired DNA of rocket scientists is focused on delivering the perfect rocket, and taking their client to the moon and back. Rarely does the rocket scientist consider the attitude or feelings of the astronaut and legions of support crews during the design and construction of the spacecraft, the launch and flight itself, and the return trip and safe recovery. Moreover, the rocket scientist may not give a thought to their day-to-day interaction with the customer during the project.

In being hired to design and build the next rocket, the customer will certainly evaluate whether it achieved its technical goals of safe space travel. But more than that, the customer will consciously or often unconsciously consider their experience with the rocket scientists on the last project, which is based on their own feelings formulated in the way they were treated. In other words, the art of human interaction plays a role, and it may be more important than the strength of the technology. Frequently, firms are viewed as being equally capable on the technical front, with the client service component being the remaining discriminator.

From our perspective, there are three dimensions of client service, which can improve sales:

- Client expectations for the way they want service delivered
- The evolution of client service over time, as a relationship matures
- How service is delivered to clients and, more importantly, how it is perceived.

Client Expectations for Service – Are you and your client compatible?

If clients come in all shapes and sizes, then why do we assume they are consistent in their expectations for client service? Gaining an understanding of a client's organization allows you to tailor your service and deliver your work in a way the client values. We believe that firms should select clients who are compatible with their overall client service delivery approach. It amazes us how little thought is invested in client selection. The act of matching clients to a firm's culture and approach to client service is often a random afterthought, with the outcome left solely to winning or losing projects advertised in business journals. Some examples of varying attitudes we have observed over the years include:

- Clients who regard themselves as either high-tech or low-tech. Some clients are openly proud of their low-tech solutions. If your firm is geared toward state-of-the-technology solutions, can you be successful in serving them?
- Many clients desire innovative approaches. In contrast, some clients are happy with industry-standard approaches, preferring to

stick with the "tried and true." Does your firm have PhDs who will turn up their noses at this client?

- While most clients today expect their phone calls returned in a reasonably timely manner, some expect ultra-responsiveness. Getting back to them this afternoon just won't cut it. Can your staff meet this expectation? In many cases, these clients are willing to pay more for this level of service.

- Some clients are cost-sensitive, while others are not. Do your firm's costs push you outside of the bell curve of the client's expectations?

- We often hear complaints that large organizations are tough to work for. Your compatibility and tolerance for bureaucracy, politics, or the disruption that typifies work with some larger clients may be worth the reward of larger project opportunities.

Part of your own selection criteria for clients should be an assessment of their overall expectations of service. How do you find this out? Simple, ask. Many clients may find it hard to put their finger on just what they want. It's sort of like trying to describe what a banana tastes like. Certainly, we know what we like when we experience it, and we also know what we don't like. Seasoned clients who have worked with many technical professionals understand and tend to better articulate their needs.

As a final note on client selection, we recommend that you quietly and discretely eliminate clients that you cannot figure out how to serve. These discussions should be closely held. Truthfully, you're doing these clients a big favor by not trying to win their future work.

Components of Client Service

The components that make up service generally include:

- <u>Technology and Innovation</u>. This is, after all, why they need you in the first place. And remember where many technically-educated clients went to school – at the same place you did. They, too, were trained to strive for the right answer, with cost and other considerations being secondary. The good news is that many of your contacts are willing to partake in lengthy, cerebral technical investigations. The bad news is that these technically-inclined folks are rarely in charge. Why? If you always placed technology first, behind budget and schedule, you might not be handed the keys to large contracts either. Nonetheless, their expectations on what will constitute the "right answer" are critical.

- Quality. This is not the same thing as *technical excellence*, and if you think so, you're headed for a tough lesson someday. Clients expect quality work as an industry norm. And all clients define quality in their own way, and will therefore have the final say. This means your calculations better be correct, double-checked, and your deliverables impeccable with no grammatical errors. That is certain. But there also will be unspoken expectations that need to be understood.

- Responsiveness. Returning calls is a common courtesy which can sometimes slip to the back-burner. Many clients express frustration at technical professionals who do not return their calls promptly. We're convinced that many technical people just don't understand how important it is. There is a tendency for technical profes-

> A universal goal of technical professionals is to arrive at the perfect solution to a problem. A new senior hire with 35 years of experience walked around before work hours, peering into cubicles and offices. He could not find a single project schedule hanging on anyone's wall. There were maps, flowcharts, aerial photographs, and certificates of recognition from prestigious societies. But there was not one schedule. He pointed out that almost every project delivered by our firm was late, some by over a year. While focusing on the perfect answer, our staff ignored deadlines. Budget overruns were chronic because time is money, after all.
>
> Technical people who hunt for the perfect answer do it selfishly. They impose their own values on the client, assuming that the importance they place on correct answers is the client's only service expectation, without thinking of the value clients place on deadlines.
>
> Many clients wish their service providers would deliver on time with answers that will work, but perhaps be less than perfectly elegant.

sionals to want to have the perfect answer before calling back. In contrast, we've observed the best consultants pick up the phone and call back immediately, even if only to listen to the client in real-time and clarify the issue. Though responsiveness takes many forms, it is uniformly valued by clients.

- <u>On time</u>. Hitting deadlines means meeting schedules not only for the end of a project, but for each intermediate milestone. Clients often have real deadlines, dictated by legal or other business considerations. Or, they might just be wired to make the trains run on time. A great many clients equate time with money and know that a late project is frequently accompanied by a budget overrun. And quality suffers during preparation of a rushed deliverable. For clients who place a high value on schedules, planning to deliver early is the only road to satisfaction.

- <u>Under Budget</u>. This refers not only to the need to stay within the bounds of your own scope and budget, but more importantly the client's overall project or program budget. Sound unfair? Perhaps, but many clients argue that the technical professional has more influence over the final outcome than they do. Hence, the pressure of meeting overall budgets.

There are a million definitions of the word "service." Keeping these categories in mind will help you to direct your conversations with client and gain an understanding of their expectations.

Levels of Client Service

Adding to the complexity of this topic, within the overall categories of client service, there is a spectrum of service levels. A good analogy might be to consider all of the different means of transportation for travelling from point A to point B. The variables for preferences might include speed, safety, cargo capacity, and comfort. The level of satisfaction for each variable will obviously differ. Selecting a pickup truck would be satisfying for someone who desires cargo capacity, but weak in comfort. On the other hand, a motorcycle would be good for someone continually in a hurry, but poor for cargo capacity. Interestingly, different people might evaluate the comfort of a motorcycle very differently, depending on personal taste, values, and preferences for style.

Likewise, levels of client service are as varied as the types of vehicles on the road. While one client may be happy to receive your deliverable in the mail, another may expect you to hand carry it to a face-to-face meeting and be briefed on the findings. Clearly, the hand-delivered version takes more work, more time, and is more costly. It's easy to see that both approaches are valid and get the job done, but differ in the *level* of service provided. Is one right, and the other wrong? Absolutely not. Could we think of additional levels of service for this example?

- The report is snail-mailed. Perhaps it's sent by courier. How about sending an administrative assistant to hand-deliver the report?
- The project manager delivers the report. Perhaps they call ahead of time to see if the client has a few minutes to receive the report and talk- maybe over lunch.
- The project manager schedules a meeting with the client and includes a few people from the project team.
- The project manager prepares an executive summary of the report and briefs staff before handing over the hardcopy draft.

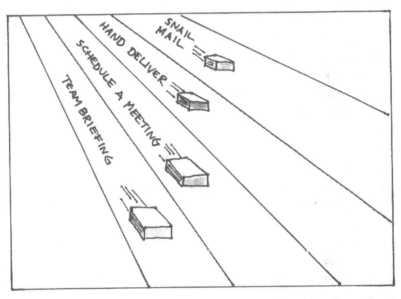

You get the point. Obviously, there are an infinite number of variations, but you see the range of potential service actions over a simple transaction of placing a deliverable into the hands of the client. Consider how varied the results (or cost) could be. At one extreme, the deliverable is snail-mailed; at the other extreme, the technical professional's entire team meets with the client and personally briefs them with a presentation. Would each and every client prefer the team briefing? Not necessarily. There is no formula for selecting the right level of service because as we have pointed out, clients vary in their preferences. Indeed even a client who may welcome a Power Point briefing under normal circumstances may prefer the deliverable be mailed if they're pressed for time. But think of the different effect these variations have on the client's perception of your level of interest in them.

There is another point to this discussion of client service *levels*. Some technical professionals wouldn't dream of thinking about the many options for getting a deliverable out the door. Many would be perfectly content to mail the report to their client, never giving it a second thought. Perhaps they're busy or they've always performed a certain way - this is perfectly understandable. Those who do take the time to weigh mailing the report against more creative ideas, such as meeting with the client, may reach a conclusion that postage saves time and expense. A more opportunistic technical professional might balance the extra cost with the benefit of client interaction and immediate feedback of their work.

We won't bore you with a discussion of low levels of service. Poor or even average service experiences leave us flat, but we often expect it in our world. High levels of service are powerful competitive differentiators to firms who achieve these lofty heights. We've all had the good fortune of being on the receiving end of terrific service by waiters, auto mechanics, retailers, or plumbers. Superior service makes most of us say "wow," and has us returning for more, telling everyone we know.

Technical professionals can achieve legendary reviews for service. There's no mystery involved, nor any secret weapon. As we've been dis-

> *Are clients willing to pay more for better service? Widely-quoted research suggests that they will, but why? Consider delivering a report to the client. It's cheaper to mail the document, compared to delivering it in person. Measured as an efficient, individual transaction, the mail is the clear choice.*
>
> *However, consider the value of hand delivering the report and providing a briefing for client staff. Though there is considerable time invested, providing this additional level of service can be more cost-effective for the client.*
>
> *If the client and staff can be briefed on the key points of the deliverable in an hour, it saves their reading every word of the report. More importantly, they'll hear all about it, as opposed to potentially not reading the document at all and remaining uninformed for the duration of the project. Also, time invested in communicating can avoid confusion and delays, which are intangible, but real benefits.*
>
> *Even if the client paid for another 3-4 hours of the project manager's time, the benefits exceed the cost.*

cussing, superior service can be the seemingly insignificant difference between mailing a report or taking the time to hand-deliver it. Quite frequently, getting the client to say "wow" is about the accumulation of many small actions.

It is not easy to achieve a reputation for superior service. Many companies strive for it because their skill sets are commodities and hence no different from their competitors. In such situations, level of service is a differentiator. If price is the only deciding factor between firms, then lowering your costs only results in eroding profit margins.

There is a widely held misconception that superior service costs more to deliver. In fact, the marginal cost for delivering better service is remarkably small in return for the premium that clients will pay to be treated well. And the sole source work that may result from satisfied clients is infinitely less expensive to procure than the long battle of responding to RFPs—it's simply a matter of investing at the correct stage of the client relationship.

Evolution of Client Service

It is helpful to observe the evolutionary development of client service over the course of an assignment. All relationships, whether personal or professional, are dynamic. And quite often there are ups and downs as client and service provider get to know one another. By recognizing these phases, you can make the best of the situation, anticipate problems, and head them off before they become serious.

- Honeymoon. Your firm has just been selected for an assignment. In the early days, there will be a honeymoon period where life is good. This is especially true if your firm has not worked for the client before, but also happens with new assignments for old friends. During this time, you almost can do no wrong because you validate the selection committee's good judgment. Also during the early stages of a project, rarely do any major or controversial issues arise, so unless you make an early blunder (we'll talk about these) life is indeed good.

- Rhythm and routine. As a project moves forward, challenging issues typically arise. Sometimes these issues are not your fault; you may be a victim of circumstances (or even a client's poor decisions). These issues can range from being relatively minor, such as a slightly missed deadline, to a major service gaffe. It's easy to misstep with a new client early in any project because you're not accustomed to working together. How your firm handles these early situations is critical because they set the tone for the rest of the project. Placing blame won't help, especially if you're foolish enough to point your finger at the client. On the other hand, if you make repairs quickly, your actions will serve you well when things really heat up.

- <u>Roller-coaster ride</u>. Eventually, most projects become a series of transactional and emotional ups and downs. Gaps emerge between the understanding reached by you and the client about the work. How does this happen, even with a detailed contract? Bear in mind that your contracted scope of work was developed during the proposal stage of your pursuit. It is reasonable to expect some differences in understanding between you and your client. In addition, as the client is exposed to your firm's means and methods of doing business, some of your weaknesses surface. The client also meets your surly receptionist, an outdated voice mail system, late or incorrect invoices, and other nuisances. On top of all this, as work begins to heat up, you may be assigned to another project or marketing pursuit, causing you to miss your deadlines. It's easy to see how client service can begin to slip.

- <u>Familiarity breeds contempt</u>. As your project nears completion, everyone begins to feel the strain of working through a series of challenges. On top of this, budget and schedule constraints eventually take center stage. As the deadline closes in, the potential for finishing late looms ominously. You may be near the end of your budget, which means that not only are you feeling the pressure from the client in delivering results, but your own management is now bearing down on you to guard against a loss. You become as tired of the client as they are of you, while working through these difficulties.

It would be easy for us to focus on happy projects, but the reality is that tough assignments are far more commonplace. Not every project unfolds in the manner listed above. What is important is to be aware of the evolution of your relationship with the client as it tracks alongside the strengths and weaknesses of your firm's client service.

Assessing Your Service

While many teams regularly assess the financial or schedule status of their assignments, they rarely take the time to request feedback on their client's feelings regarding the service being provided. You should always know where you stand with clients. Is it solid ground or quicksand? Here are some examples of the range of situations project teams can find themselves in:

- <u>Average – Business as usual</u>. Generally speaking, things are ok. The client is fine with your approach, and has nothing major to complain about, but also nothing to be overly excited about. You're in a state of dynamic equilibrium with the client, and while there are no threats to your relationship, there also doesn't seem to be anything to make them do handsprings, either. You can continue in this manner, provided a motivated competitor doesn't become interested in stealing them away.

- <u>Below Average - Mixed reviews</u>. There are a few rough spots. The client may acknowledge that a difficult project has inherent tension, and that "ups and downs" are expected. But look out for signs that nerves are wearing thin. There is no need to push the panic button-- yet. The firm's leadership often is unaware of the situation, and therefore misses an opportunity to improve the relationship. You should be looking to better understand the source of the rough spots, and make adjustments in your approach. Fortunately, with a concerted effort, you have a chance to save your firm's relationship with the client. Look for opportunities to show improvement.

- <u>Poor – Thin ice</u>. You're not going to win the next assignment, and you may not get to finish the work you've started. The only thing protecting you at this point is the client's desire to avoid the delays and costs associated with changing firms. Management intervention is needed, with direct involvement by senior leadership. Reaching the brink of being fired is more often an accumulation of many small errors than a single cataclysmic event. Sadly, your plight may not be reversible, once you've reached this point, and your trip to the penalty box could be measured in years. Although experience shows that clients are more understanding than most people think, the one piece of advice we can offer is to not get to this point—anticipate and respond to the declining relationship.

- <u>Above Average – Life is good</u>. If your clients are rating your level of service above the average of all of their experiences with technical professionals including your competitors, then you've inherited a competitive advantage. You and members of your team are doing more things right and few bad things. When asked, your client gives you good grades for your work and your delivery. You should be sharing lessons-learned with the rest of your firm by communicating what you are doing, as an example of effective client service.

- <u>Excellent - Ecstatic</u>. This is a great place to be, because your firm and your team are running like a Swiss watch. We find that technical professionals who provide excellent client service have several common attributes. They all know how to anticipate the client's problems, and they tailor their approach to meet the client's preferences. They make recommendations on how to deal with problems before they become significant, and proactively take action. As a result of this level of appreciation for your service, you're the automatic front-runner for future assignments, and may receive a large share of their new work without serious competition. The client easily justifies awarding you more work because of the added value you bring, technically and personally.

- <u>Superior - Legendary</u>. Few firms achieve this lofty plateau, but if they do, then the rewards are plentiful. Clients will reach for the phone to contact their colleagues and urge them to hire your firm. This is the platinum standard, and you'll be able to charge a premium for your services because of the added value. Interestingly, we find that many technical professionals are dubious that this position can even be reached, or that it might be worth attaining. Our observation is that legendary service cannot be imagined; it must be experienced.

Obtaining Client Service Performance Feedback

If all this discussion about client expectations, levels of client service, and the evolution of client relationships over time has your head spinning, we are not surprised. You didn't learn about this in your calculus, chemistry or engineering class. Although it is difficult to ask clients how they would like to be served, because they often do not know, if you pose the right questions, you can obtain good results.

There are two main components of client service performance feedback. The first is to find out what your clients value. The second is to find out how you're doing. This information, taken together, will allow you to objectively evaluate your client service program using real data on how your clients feel. It will enable you to adjust and improve your service, tailored to the preferences of your clients.

Methods for Obtaining Feedback

Textbooks are filled with methods for measuring client satisfaction, but we find that most of them refer to consumer goods and services, especially new product test marketing. There is little direct application to technical services firms, which are unique because of the complex, yet very individualized, nature of the service they deliver. Common methods applicable to our industry include:

- <u>Routine direct feedback.</u> The best feedback is obtained day-to-day, during the normal course of performing work. However obvious it may seem, many technical professionals don't think about their client service, instead being consumed by project details. This is understandable, but inexcusable. With many clients, a simple, "how are we doing?" asked in a private moment often generates an invaluable response. One suggestion to help you remember client service is to add it to the agenda of your regular project meetings. This reminder serves both the project team and the client. Incumbent service providers have an inherent advantage over newcomers because of improved access to client feedback. You do not want to lose this edge.

- <u>Project team reports</u>. Different people see and hear different things. Many times, the look on a client's face will speak volumes. However, a busy Project Manager who is running client meetings, consumed by details, and taking notes can easily miss important signs. We recommend that internal project meetings include discussion of the team's observations from "reading" the client.

- <u>Independent client audits</u>. Many managers are card-carrying optimists; they assume that all clients are pleased with the firm's work. We know, statistically, that no firm is perfect. You are performing a disservice to your teams if you don't help them obtain objective feedback. Sometimes known as "wellness checks," many firms send senior staff to talk to clients about performance. We've found that almost all clients genuinely appreciate this type of meeting, especially if it's from the company's Chief Executive. Obviously, for larger firms, this becomes a time management challenge for the boss.

An important caveat to this approach is that the individual conducting the independent audit must remain objective. Defensiveness can irritate the client. The auditor must make it clear to the customer that they want the straight story, no matter how tough it may be to hear.

- Postcard/e-mail surveys. Mass-mailed surveys can be conducted for technical services firms, much as they are used for consumer goods. Though some would argue that this faceless approach is the antithesis of client interaction, there is a place for this method. They are a fairly inexpensive means to solicit feedback. Unfortunately, the response rate can be quite low because the average person is inundated with them at each restaurant, hotel, and car dealership they visit. The advent of internet-based surveys also has crowded this field. A limitation of this form of soliciting feedback is that it provides little opportunity for clarification or follow-up. Typically, the survey is structured for "yes" or "no" answers, or for a numeric rating. These work well for compiling statistical trends, but offer limited opportunity for important commentary. Positive or negative feedback can be flagged for special attention, such as a face-to-face visit.

- Telephone surveys. If you're rolling your eyes at the thought of a telemarketer interrupting your client's dinner, don't be alarmed. If done well, phone interviews with clients can be cost-effective and obtain valuable feedback. However, it is critical that these calls be requested and scheduled in advance and permission granted before proceeding. Consent can be obtained through a simple e-mail from the president, requesting permission to participate. We have found the response rate to be quite high, even 100%, when clients are approached in this manner. Questions for guiding the telephone interview should be prepared in advance to ensure a common structure for comparing responses. We've found that marketing staff perform very well in conducting phone interviews. They have a solid background in sales, are good listeners, and have no vested interest in a particular technology.

Ongoing measurement of client satisfaction should be integral to your firm's quality management program. Ensuring technical excellence is a cornerstone activity for well-run firms and should be managed by top leadership.

Our recommendations:

- Measure with multiple techniques. Use more than one of the techniques identified above. A diversity of approaches to measuring customer feedback increases assurance of ferreting out both favorable and unfavorable responses.

- Aim for comprehensive measurement. Try to obtain coverage from all of your firm's customers. For larger firms, we recognize the challenge of the numbers, but some techniques can be applied cost-effectively across broad populations. This ensures that no one falls through the cracks and that a small client service issue doesn't develop into a full-fledged company problem just because you were not aware of it.

- Focus management attention on key accounts. Your leadership's primary emphasis should be on key accounts. Work with your accounting staff to determine the clients who provide the majority of your revenue and profit (typically, 20% of your clients provide 80% of your revenue). Simply begin at the top, then work your way down the list— an effective approach to prioritizing your leadership's attention.

- Break down feedback by geographic groups or business lines. Evaluate key clients in each of the segments of your organization. This balances input from important customers in all divisions that you measure performance. Sorting and re-sorting information can illuminate areas of your business that are not getting attention.

- Consider targeted surveys. Specially purposed outreach programs are excellent. Client service feedback can be readily obtained in conjunction with other strategic and tactical initiatives. As an example, we conducted a successful branding exercise in which marketing coordinators spoke with clients about their overall impressions of the firm.

- Deal with known issues. It's critical to deal with client service issues identified during assessments! Follow-up by company leadership is the reason behind the entire effort of obtaining feedback.

Management should be completely engaged, with the intent of hastening your exit out of the penalty box. A major reason for failure of a survey program is when the client feels you aren't listening. If you don't follow up, and don't make changes, it will reinforce the sense that they are wasting their time providing input.

One of the fundamental tenets of this book is that there is no substitute for seeing clients face-to-face and talking to them. Asking them on a regular basis about your level of client service can only improve your firm's prospects for successful projects and winning new work.

Planning Your Client Service Approach

We find that most individuals and firms don't really think about tailoring their service to the unique needs and desires of a given client. This is fascinating in light of the fact that many clients are willing to pay more for better service. Our recommendation: consider matching a client's needs for service with their needs for a technical solution. This requires conscious thinking about what the client values and how to craft your delivery.

We recommend that every firm plan their approach to achieving the desired level of service for each client. Once decided, be sure to communicate it to staff. If necessary, provide training to staff in the actions that define superior client service. Everyone from the word processors to the accountants to the managers needs to understand clearly their role in the service line. Actions taken to achieve high levels of client service often require empowerment from management to "do what's right" for the client.

From a competitive perspective, it is paramount to reinforce the idea that not all clients are looking for the same type of service from their technical professionals. Providing good client service is not a competitive differentiator because it is an expected industry norm. On the other hand, superior service can put you over the top of your competition, even though it may not be a stated evaluation criterion in the selection process.

In addition to teaching your organization how to identify and emulate superior service, it's important to recognize the points at which client service can go awry.

Common Pitfalls of Client Service

There are several pitfalls, often repeated by technical professionals, which lead to mistakes in client service. You can not only upset your client, but also your boss. Imagine being caught in the middle of two upset parties in these examples:

- Slow start. One of the most common early mistakes on a project is a slow start. Why does this happen? Project teams in technical service firms often juggle multiple commitments. While working on proposals for their next project, they sometimes set aside their current commitments. As they begin to catch up, the new project is ramping up. Ideally, the project team seeks to meet or beat their deadline for the new engagement, which compounds the pressure. With multiple commitments, it is vitally important to start on the right foot or you will find yourself playing constant catch-up, possibly for the entire project.

- Key personnel changes. Project teams change their roster for a wide range of reasons. However, making a major change in your team too soon,

> One of the greatest sources of client service friction is a technical disagreement. Technical professionals are naturally wired to seek the perfect answer. In their world, there is only one right answer, bound by the harmonious intersection of physics, chemistry, and economics. However, client decision-making is often also governed by personal preferences, politics, budget, and schedule.
>
> A common source of dispute occurs when a technical professional draws a conclusion based solely on their own perspective. In their heart, they believe they've thoroughly analyzed the client's need and their answer is the right one. Then, as they present their ideas at a client meeting, they're ambushed over priorities which were never considered.
>
> After some heated discussion, an impasse is reached when the technical professional stubbornly digs in. The client becomes frustrated because they're paying good money for advice, but their provider isn't listening.
>
> This really boils down to the relationship with the client, gaining perspective, listening, offering choices, and putting the client's preferences before your own. It's also a reminder that technical professionals need to recognize there is more than one right answer.

especially for the Project Manager, can be a real client service set-back. Clients refer to this as a "bait and switch," and sometimes guard against it by contractually binding key personnel during negotiations. If you must make changes, discuss them with the client in advance and be prepared to substitute individuals with equally strong credentials.

- Scope and budget conflicts. This topic can be one of the greatest sources of client service problems. It is common for scope or schedule conflicts to crop up early, especially if the statements in your proposal, written in haste to meet the deadline, become language in your contract. Clients rightfully hold us accountable, but proposals are sales documents. In reality, much discussion needs to take place before defining a binding covenant between your firm and the client. If you're faced with a client who immediately sends you a contract with your proposal attached to be signed, request a meeting to slow things down and discuss the scope of work. It is worthwhile to review each point to ensure a common understanding of the work.

> *Superior client service requires clear understanding of roles and responsibilities within a firm, especially limits of authority. Time-critical situations, such as a client service error, demand immediate action. Many errors can be corrected on the spot, before they grow. More complex problems might call for management involvement to resolve a client's concerns. Keep in mind that time is of the essence.*
>
> *It's difficult to adequately document policies and procedures which anticipate all potential client service errors. We recommend instead conducting training that use case studies as an effective method for teaching technical professionals. Management can establish a positive environment of focusing on fixing client service problems first, then asking questions later.*

- Breaking bad news. Red wines improve with age. Unfortunately, bad news about problems on a project does not. In fact, the longer you procrastinate to bring bad news to the attention of your client, the better the chances that your client will hear it from someone else. So, we'll state the obvious and strongly urge you to disclose issues early. Be prepared to apologize right away. This not only worked in elementary school, but it works with your clients. And, it goes without saying that bringing potential solutions is essential.

- Invoicing errors. Invoices are as much a deliverable as your technical reports. But imagine your invoices arriving late and filled with errors. This can be a major client service problem because it deals with money- a lightning rod for client headaches. Obviously, strive for on-time, error-free invoices, and don't learn through trial and error how your client wants them formatted. One successful approach is to prepare a draft invoice, then sit down with the client's accounts payable staff to review the format and content, and understand their deadlines for internal approvals and check runs. Late invoices run a risk of being received after deadlines for encumbered funds have lapsed, especially dangerous when there are restrictions on budgets being carried forward to the next fiscal year.

- Not providing alternatives for the client. One of the great delusions of even the most seasoned technical professionals is that they assume that when they have sized up a situation, done the math, formulated the options, and developed a recommendation, the client will simply and logically agree. Everyone likes to have choices, even if they're all relatively unattractive. Being presented with at least two options, allows a client to make a choice. In some cases, your direct client won't have the final say, deferring to an executive team or city council. Technical professionals must recognize that these people exist to make decisions. So, give them two or more choices, then help them understand their options. But under no circumstances should you paint your client into a corner by not providing them choices from which they can make a decision.

- Personality conflicts. If you find that your project is gradually becoming more difficult, and you begin to think that a "personality conflict" is to blame, take notice. It's likely that you or members of your project team aren't quite getting it right. While there may not be a major problem, chronic dissatisfaction with day-to-day activities can easily grow out of control. If you sense this is the case, then consider making half-time adjustments to your game plan. It would be a good time to arrange for client feedback from an independent observer. Look for opportunities to improve on the little things, as they can add up, as opposed to trying to make wholesale changes.

- <u>Project team attitude</u>. What happens when members of your project team are overworked, under-appreciated, and upset? While it is very easy to be consumed by technical and management details, the health and well-being of your project team needs attention too. Be sure to step back now and then, and ask them how they're doing. Some of the worst incidents we've seen are the airing of the company's dirty laundry to a client. It is important to reinforce and reward good client service behavior among your team members as it is to deal with client service errors caused by them.

- <u>Problem anticipation</u>. Frequently cited during client feedback surveys, the difference between good and great service is the ability to anticipate a client's problems and to recommend solutions. While most clients appreciate common courtesy and responsiveness, more significant is the ability to consider the future and help your client foresee issues. Clients are quick to point out that a technical professional can cement a relationship by proactively thinking through courses of action. One good way to do this is in monthly reports, by identifying "areas of concern" or "upcoming issues." Another approach is to set aside time during project meetings to specifically consider project risks and the means of managing their outcome.

- <u>Asking for more money</u>. Project change orders may be one of the toughest client service challenges of all, but they are common. There are good and bad reasons for running out of budget, so the first thing to do is to size up why you might need more money. First, get your facts straight. Scour the project management accounting reports, evaluate the contracted scope, and determine the financial status of the project.

    Second, take responsibility for your actions and decisions. If you've overrun the budget because you used inexperienced staff and trained them on the client's budget, or because of sheer ineptitude, then eat the overrun. Making clients pay for poor management is indefensible. In addition, you'll make up the difference in the long run, as clients will be more forgiving of unanticipated problems or mistakes of their own making.

Third, meet with the client as soon as possible and be prepared to answer their questions. They will ask you when you first learned of the problem and will take a dim view of your not addressing it immediately.

Look for options to mitigate damages. Clients often are willing to downsize the scope or eliminate tasks altogether in order to stay within a prescribed budget. While this approach won't work in every situation, it is worth considering. Some clients may ask that you settle all budget issues at the end of the contract. This has some risks, so carefully document budget requests in writing throughout the project, to protect your firm and yourself. We've seen cases where the firm made the decision to wait on budget requests without consulting the client. In many instances, the client's hands are tied at the end of the project, and will be unable to authorize additional funds, even if they want to.

> *If you're a client, do you think about the level of service you desire and whether it can tip the scales in your selection process? Or do you use your scoring spreadsheets, without considering the competitor's service approach?*
>
> *A major Federal agency has a reputation for being biased toward incumbents – completely by design. We discussed this with a representative, and they openly admitted it. They believe that past performance is an indication of future results. Firms who have worked for them in the past also know their standards, approach, and unique needs. New firms would have to learn all of that, taking more time and money.*
>
> *For clients, we suggest you decide what kind of service you would like and select firms who deliver it. For marketers, consider this point wisely. This isn't about having the best technology, rather it's about tailoring service to fit the client's preferences.*

Preparing for the Next Procurement

If you're a client, you may be thinking that all this discussion about service seems a little artificial. One could easily get the feeling that service providers are being nice only because they selfishly want to win the next assignment. The fact is that service is our profession. All firms strive to establish long-term, trust-based relationships that lead to repeat business (which, again, is the lowest cost way to procure new business.)

To the service providers, we recommend you always act as if there is another major procurement right around the corner, because there always will be; if not for your current client, then for another with whom they may share their experiences.

We know that clients take service into consideration when deciding the outcome of sole source and competitive selections for new work, though the criterion often is hidden from plain sight. We rarely hear clients request a "client service approach." Instead, we hear that "experience" gave the winning team an edge because they knew how to "work with" the client's organization to get things done. In contrast, rarely do we hear that one firm's technology was superior as the deciding reason.

During positioning for a pursuit with a current client, your history of service with them must be addressed. If your firm has done a good job in providing great client service, then your positioning activities will be easier. Unfortunately, not every pursuit will be that easy. Realistically, you'll need to deal with the ups and downs of your service.

When dealing with clients for whom you have never worked, stating that your firm provides great service could be a mistake. It is likely to come across as self-serving without the proof to back it up. The most effective approach we've seen is to let your actions speak louder than your words, by offering evidence of successful past performance. Referrals or testimonials from satisfied clients may be one of the best proofs of successful client service. After all, clients tend to trust one another. If you handle this correctly, you may be able to get a boost from a long-time client. You can even offer to draft the referral letter to get the ball rolling. And no, you're not being presumptuous; clients won't blindly put their name on letters they don't mean.

Testimonials should also be targeted. If your new pursuit deals with operations and maintenance, then a quote from the plant or system superintendent might be stronger than one obtained from the Chief Financial Officer.

Other evidence that provides indirect proof of good client service includes using data that compares final project costs or schedule to original estimates.

As a final word on presenting your case as an effective service provider, you will still find it challenging to overcome an incumbent. There is just no substitute for the strong personal relationships formed on the foundation of a track record of successful service. Hence, we urge you and your firm to focus on continuous improvement in client service.

The Role of a Client Service Manager

Many firms appoint Client Service Managers (CSMs) to be their key leaders in serving clients. In earlier days, this position may have been called client managers. This title has been dropped because service providers don't really *manage* clients; rather they manage the *service* provided to clients. In most firms, a given CSM is likely to serve more than one client, perhaps four or five. Some large clients with complex organizations may require the focus of an entire team of CSMs.

Historically, technical services firms served clients by assigning company management to oversee the activities. As firms grew into more complex businesses, this approach stretched the limits of top management. More individuals were needed to cover the gap. Today, client service responsibility is often more evenly distributed across firms, with staff adding client service management to their technical and management duties.

Acting as a CSM puts you in the driver's seat of a number of activities. First and foremost, you assume ownership of all obligations and interactions between your company and the client. If this sounds like a lot of responsibility, it is. You'll be overseeing delivery of all services, solutions and work products to the client. In some cases, you may be managing or conducting the work yourself. But in most instances, you'll be looking after work done by others. This requires you not only to keep an eye on expected tasks and activities, but also to anticipate impending doom and to take care of issues before they become problems. As you can imagine, being a CSM can be a tough assignment, but it can also be highly rewarding. As CSM you will be situated for recognition of a job well done. In addition, you'll be a direct link in the "food chain," where advancement and reward are likely.

To accomplish all that is required, CSMs must form client service teams. CSM team leaders recognize that some of their team members may also be serving other clients, and are obligated to other CSMs in the firm. As a CSM team leader, you may also have roles on other teams. CSMs also take the lead in succession planning, by grooming and training replacements for themselves.

CSMs are responsible for understanding their client's business and full range of needs for technical professional services. They maintain a current understanding of external or internal drivers which form the basis of those needs. CSMs are able to identify opportunities to provide service or solutions, leading to continuous work for the firm. CSMs should be mindful of, and focus on, those strategic opportunities which enable both the client and the technical professional services firm to simultaneously achieve strategic goals.

In addition, the CSM builds an understanding of the client's organization and decision-making process. By developing and maintaining relationships with key individuals at the staff, management and political levels, the CSM can gain a better appreciation for their client's needs. CSMs also work to create solutions to meet needs for which the client might not even be aware. This might result in a new assignment, perhaps awarded sole source.

Experienced CSMs always seem to find a way to provide whatever service is required to meet their client's need, and take full responsibility for quality results, even if outside firms or subcontractors perform the work.

If you have been in the business for a few years, you've probably experienced more than one client service failure. As we've outlined in this chapter, they can happen for any number of reasons. Sometimes, combinations of circumstances contribute to a perfect storm in which the entire relationship with a client goes up in flames. Regardless of the cause, have you ever wondered how and why events conspired to cause collapse? There are often many clues.

In our experience, these unfortunate cases almost always have one condition in common – lack of a strong, engaged CSM. It's easy for technical professionals to become preoccupied with tasks or activities. Moreover, there are numerous outside influences which can magnify day-to-day challenges.

We're fond of saying that it's easy to think of a hundred things that can go wrong, but only limited conditions for success. The primary role of a CSM is to be the first line of defense against a client service breakdown. In other words, if you're a CSM, the buck stops with you.

Good CSMs anticipate service problems before they occur and deal with conditions that may cause issues to erupt. Problems do occur, and as a CSM, your job is to take ownership— the one who looks out for the client and the interests of the firm.

The Importance of Client Service Management as a Profession

There is growing industry-wide recognition of the importance of client service management. We have found the greatest appeal of being a CSM is being externally focused and spending time with clients. A well-rounded career sees tours of duty in building technical skills, sales skills, and client service skill, on a rotating basis. They perfectly complement each other.

Serving clients should be revered; if your firm sees this differently, you should seriously question its values. In many firms, CSMs are seated at the head of the table, and the office manager serves them. The CSM should have clout within your firm, able to move mountains to serve clients. CSMs should be well-rewarded for delivering revenue, profit, sales, repeat business, and providing oversight of the firm's services and solutions. Many firms recognize the importance of CSMs by making them the most highly paid people in their organization. Managers should provide a great deal of attention to CSMs.

> *Back to the client service challenge, I asked our team if we could remedy our problems to turn around our relationship with the client's staff. The immediate response was no, because the general contractor had been paid, and the job had been closed out long ago. Even the warranty period for plant equipment had expired. At this point, I asked the group how much they thought it would cost to fix the problems. After a brief huddle the repairs were estimated to be around $5,000, total. So I asked if we could spend our own money to hire a contractor to tighten the bolts at the pump station, patch the parking lot asphalt, and seal the roof leaks. The attendees asked, "Can we do that? Is it legal? Will management let us?" After a few minutes of debate, we agreed to go ahead.*
>
> *Weeks later, we received the anticipated RFP for the major plant expansion. We wrote a proposal, attended an interview, and we were selected for $5 million worth of engineering work. The compelling feedback from the selection committee was that our firm stood by its work, and could be trusted to make things right. While spending $5,000 out of our own pocket on client service was not a routine occurrence, it sure made a difference.*

Chapter 6
The Attributes of Successful Business Developers and Marketers

People should be judged on the basis of their performance,
not nationality, personality, education, or personal traits and skills.
- Marvin Bower, businessman & author

Your boss comes into your office. He tells you the firm needs to hire another person to develop new business. "The market's ripe, it's time to grow. Find somebody good," he says. You say what you always say when the boss comes around, "Sure, no problem."

You have never hired anyone, but you have common sense, don't you? Your first thought is to post an ad on Craigslist. It reads: Wanted. Personable, experienced marketer to support new technical sales. Click. Within two weeks, 600 resumes sit in a stack on your desk.

You sort the resumes into piles. On one corner of your desk, all the people with 10 plus years of experience. On the other corner, all the applicants from firms you most respect. Pretty soon, you have forty piles of paper on your desk, a mess. Every resume looks reasonable in some way, though how can you tell? How do you know if these people are as good as they say they are?

You throw your hands up, then plead to the acoustical ceiling in your office for help...

What does a successful business developer look like?

Every organization needs business developers. They are the motors that drive every other part of any business. What separates the technical services industry from most others is that rather than using non-technical sales people, we ask technical staff members to lead the sales process, since their talent and effort are the "products" being sold.

Though many firms have sales training programs, more often than not we see a process of either encouraging or discouraging staff members from spending time on sales, based on the quality of their performance. If they are successful at winning work, they are typically asked to spend a greater amount of time doing it. If they aren't, they are asked to invest less, and to instead stay in the office and develop their technical skills.

Most firms are in constant need of new business development staff. The chicken-and-the-egg question is: are talented sales staff born or trained? Do you focus on hiring staff with that talent or do you train your staff from within your organization? The answer, of course, is both. A firm needs to work both sides of the equation-- hire staff externally (which has the added benefit of infusing a company with new ideas) and develop staff internally. Investing time in understanding the attributes of a successful business developer will result in an increased ability to:

- Identify the technical people in your firm that you should train in the techniques of business development, and
- Identify and hire new sales-oriented staff.

So, what does a good business developer or marketer look like? The negative connotations of the word salesperson complicate the identification of the positive aspects of the role. The technical services salesperson is a mix of characteristics, talents, and goals—a blend of rocket scientist and artist. It's difficult to find individuals who combine both characteristics. However, we've met a number of people who work comfortably in both sets of shoes. Business developers come in every size, shape, and type. Of course, you know the BD person who can memorize every name in the room, or the one who can squeeze information out of any recalcitrant contracting agent. Those are obvious. But for every superstar, we know dozens of sales geniuses who defy typecasting, yet are equally successful. Some are modest, quiet, hardly say anything at the office, but they always return from business trips with million dollar contracts. Why are they successful? Many of these traits can be learned, but most are innate to a person's character.

- **Empathetic**— great business developers care about the challenges people face and they have a natural desire to help. They show a natural interest in others, which leads them to ask questions. Understanding another person's problems leads to creating a trusting partnership with them, centered on common interests.
- **Competitive**— successful business developers enjoy winning work. They are the people that make one extra phone call, write

one more draft of the proposal, and prepare for one extra hour before an interview. That's what sets them apart—they want to win.

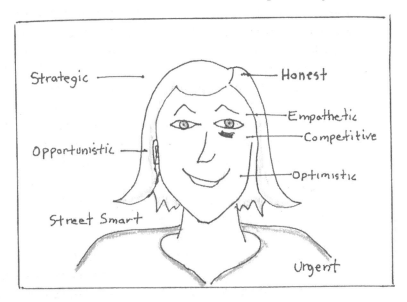

- **Strategic**— most great business developers think strategically about the pursuit of new work. Like great chess players, they strategize several moves ahead of their current position. It provides them with constant momentum. They know the steps that will lead to successful selection and they know how to sidestep the competition's efforts. They may also work harder than anyone, but they set themselves apart by working smarter than everyone.
- **Optimistically Opportunistic**— much has been made of people who see the glass half full. More so, great business developers envision opportunities where mere mortals only see the immediate project in front of them. Their sense of timing is acute, acting speedily to position their firm for the best possible outcome for a current project, AND for the subsequent programs that tumble out.
- **Street-smart**— we are tempted to say that great business developers have a lot of common sense. This is certainly true, but it understates their business prowess. Great business developers can cut through the fog of technical details and politics and see

complex issues with clarity. There is no substitute for hard-won experience, coupled with savvy.

- **Urgent**— most importantly, the one characteristic of a great business developer that sets them apart is their overriding sense of URGENCY. They're not impatient, they're not desperate, but they approach work every day with a sense of urgency. That part of their personality makes them move constantly toward closing the deal, moving every conversation toward an inevitable contract. These are people who never give up. They overcome long odds by continually finding new ways to win. Their stamina gives them an advantage, enabling them to outlast the competition. Some have been known to pursue a sale for ten years or more.
- **Honest**— It is worth a mention that the profession features access to sensitive information. A person you can trust is crucial.

In our experience, these are the traits that successful business developers share. Of course, you often have to contend with other aspects of their personalities, sometimes including oversized egos and embarrassing selfishness. But no one's perfect. And a salesperson with a well-fed ego often has justification. They win work, a lot of it, and they want you to know it. We can live with that.

The Qualities of a Successful Non-Technical Marketer

Non-technical marketing support staff work in partnership with the technical staff to achieve a company's business development goals. Quality marketing staff members share many of the same attributes of the business developer that are described above. But they also offer other qualities that are complementary to those of the business developer, making them valuable partners. These people are:

- **Organized**— similar to sports in which body control equals ball control, an organized person is the foundation of an organized pursuit. A naturally organized marketer carefully stacks the building blocks of a proposal to build a logical and persuasive argument. A competitive proposal provides complex information to potential clients. The number one responsibility of a marketer is to tend the development and harvesting of information with the same care as a farmer tends an acre of corn.

- **Parallel Processors**— a good marketer will always be involved in numerous pursuits simultaneously, all at different levels of gestation (see sidebar). The ability to push assignments forward, moving from one to other, is an important characteristic of a talented worker in any industry. But in the marketing department of a busy technical services office, it's the engine that drives the bus. A firm has to be able to efficiently deliver proposals that win the work to thrive and grow.

- **Clear Thinking**— marketing staff are bombarded by demands from all directions. At the same time, there are multiple tiers of issues to be resolved, ranging from the mundane (what type of paper should I use?), to the profound (we are well-positioned to win a pending major oppor-

When hiring marketing support staff, we suggest looking at their resume for past experience at a restaurant. Before arriving on the doorstep of technical services, we both served food to hungry people. There's no better training for supporting technical staff.

A food server learns to work well in a fast-paced environment that demands teamwork among a variety of people with differing priorities (managers, busboys, cooks, hostesses). Food service workers develop strong camaraderie from surviving Mother's Day brunch. A good waitperson is often challenged to attempt to please people who cannot be pleased. They can smile when they want to say, "go jump in the lake," because they know where their tips are coming from.

Food servers are good managers of customer dining experiences. They can multi-task, thinking holistically about their tables, moving each table's meal forward a little at a time-- an appetizer here, a dessert over there, gliding from table to table. Most importantly, they are cool under fire.

Through these experiences we learned many skills. One vivid lesson: you cannot please everyone, no matter how hard you try. If 500 people walk into a restaurant or dining hall, at least one of them will be dissatisfied. The soup will be cold, there won't be enough chicken in their pot pie, or wine will be spilled. The goal of a service provider is not to eliminate mistakes or accidents, but to respond to them with a strategy to make even a wine spill a positive memory in the mind of the customer.

tunity, but our proposed project manager can't make it to the interview). The ability to sort through and prioritize a myriad of activities is highly valued in marketing staff. Valued individuals have a knack for seeing through the clutter in a world of multiple challenges, then clearly thinking of the right thing to do, and doing it.

- **Cool demeanor**— providing marketing support for a technical services firm is a pressure-filled job. Any project performed under a deadline, with a variety of people involved, and in which you have limited control, is a recipe for conflict. A marketer who can travel through this process, while maintaining emotional equilibrium, is priceless. You cannot underestimate how the emotional highs and lows of a marketer affect everyone working on the pursuit and the overall mood of the team.

When we think back to the memorable business developers and marketers we've worked with, what stands out is that they knew how to work with groups of people. They saw everyone as partners, knowing that each person is a key player in getting a proposal out the door. Too many BD people are "lone rangers" and make people around them feel unimportant. As a result, they never have a team of people who are willing to make the extra effort, so they are ultimately less efficient and less successful.

When talented BD and marketing staff are elevated into leadership positions, they use their innate talents, as described above, to rally the troops and turn pursuits into memorable efforts. Rarely do these individuals need to lead by "command and control." However, if the conditions call for it, they have no problem using their authority to achieve results. Much of the time, they bring people together through making compelling points via reasoning, logic, and relating their own experiences. When called upon, they have personality attributes which allow them to command respect under fire. Teams under their leadership follow their direction willingly because of confidence and respect for their judgment.

Business developers should spend the majority of their time developing relationships with potential clients; marketers should be their partners in delivering persuasive sales documents to prospective clients. Finding the right mix of talent and personality for each of these members of the team is a critical component of a sales program.

Finding and Hiring Business Developers and Marketing Staff

Building a successful sales program starts with hiring the right people. No marketing program can achieve its intended goals without sales and marketing professionals who have the attributes described in the previous section.

Technical professional services firms face labor-intensive, highly competitive marketing challenges. Your firm will always need people who can implement a strategic pursuit, as well as marketing staff who can organize, write, edit, manage, and deliver compelling and persuasive sales documents.

Warning: we've hired people who walked on water in the interview, then sank under the waves after a few months. We've hired people against our instincts who became wildly successful. Hiring is as much a roll of the dice as some RFPs you decide to pursue.

Follow the advice in the epigraph at the beginning of this chapter. Personality traits and attributes are important, but meeting goals is the true measure of success.

Provide your staff with clearly defined metrics and expectations, a reasonable timeframe to show results, and all the support you can provide, then measure, discuss, communicate, and refine your organization based on results.

Trust is important, but your organization's mantra should be "show me."

The process of hiring should be as well organized as the process of pursuing a major contract. They're very similar. In both cases, you're selling the firm's differentiators to a buyer, you're assessing whether the relationship between you and the buyer is a good fit, and you're negotiating financial terms. A good manager of a major campaign will also be a good hiring manager. The first mistake many firms make is to put someone in charge of hiring who does not have the right temperament to sell the firm or the position that is offered. A good salesperson should be in charge of hiring a good salesperson.

In the previous sidebar, we told you one of the key questions to ask to a potential marketing person, "Did you ever wait tables at a restaurant?" But there are a number of other questions and a few lessons we've learned over the years to seek out new staff, select them, and bring them onboard.

First: Assess. It may seem obvious to say that first you should assess the needs of your organization, but many firms move quickly to hire into a new position or to replace departed staff without taking the time to determine the best type of position or replacement. It is essential to determine the best fit for the strategic goals you want to achieve. Hiring a salesperson to grow an office from 2 people to 25 takes someone with an entrepreneurial streak, who doesn't mind answering their own phone. That same person hired to "maintain" a longstanding client in an office of 300 people may end up being bored and feeling like "one of the crowd."

Similarly, when a marketing coordinator with 5 years of experience resigns, do you instinctively hire a replacement with similar skills and experience? Not necessarily. A marketing department must have the right balance of talent and experience. You must respond to immediate needs, but also envision how your department should look in three years. Hiring a new college graduate, for example, may be more cost-effective and can bring energy into a lackluster organization, if you have the freedom to be patient and get them up to speed.

An often posed question by the leaders of services firms to their directors of business development is, "Why do we have so many Marketing people?" Every organization should have a motivating drive to "maximize sales and minimize cost." But it is challenging to know where those curves intersect. Twenty marketing coordinators can produce twice as many proposals as ten, but cost twice as much. Is it a zero-sum game? Not necessarily. Anyone involved in sales knows that doubling opportunities does not automatically double sales.

A couple rules of thumb: 1) the more business developers you hire for competitive markets, the more you need to assure they are supported by skilled marketing staff. The partnership between the two groups is a critical factor in efficiency, allowing the BD people to commit more time out of the office with clients and allowing the marketing people to take advantage of the sales opportunities that are being generated. 2) It takes nearly as much time to write a proposal for a $100,000 project as for a $1,000,000 project. Clients expect a scope of work, project experience, resumes, and other information for all of them. A good marketer can work on 2-3 projects simultaneously, but suddenly ramping up their workload will stress them and the overall system. Ramping up the value of the pursuit is a better way to increase sales in the long run, rather than simply pursuing more projects.

<u>Second: Organize</u>. A well-crafted advertisement that sells the firm is a must. Job descriptions tend to become repositories for everyone's input on the position, swelling to 4-5 pages. No one could live up to them. Allow your marketers to give your stale advertisements a tune-up, and be open to modifying the position, based on the quality of the people you are interviewing. Cast a wide net. Considering applicants from outside of the industry is a gamble, but can pay off enormously, if the selected person brings an infusion of new ideas.

Resumes of all types will arrive on your desk. The sorting and winnowing of applicants is a process in which all business developers and marketers should participate at some point in their careers. Why? Because it's the closest they'll ever get to being in a client's shoes. There are several similarities in the selection process that provide insight into our own BD challenges (and also sympathy for our clients). These include:

- **Advertising**: you can see the challenge of developing a well-written job announcement, which shows how hard it is for clients to write a good Request for Proposals. One or two poorly worded phrases can introduce misinterpretation and confusion.

- **Sorting through a multitude of well qualified candidates**: you shouldn't be surprised to receive dozens of resumes from applicants with degrees from respected schools and experience as formidable competitors. You see the challenge in developing selection criteria that allow the most qualified to emerge as the chosen firm. There's a fine balance between highly subjective judging criteria versus overly complex mathematical scoring systems.

- **Interviewing**: Participating in a recruiting process for a staff member provides insight into why clients often have a two-phase process of requesting information, then requiring an in-person interview. What looks good on paper can fall apart in person. It's a reminder of the importance of the interview phase in our BD efforts.

<u>Third: Facilitate the shortlist and interview process.</u> We highly recommend empowering an interview panel that is representative of the people the business developer or marketer will serve. Inclusion of these people provides a cross section of perspectives and makes the interview panel accountable for their decision. They will take ownership of their decision and work toward making that person successful.

Look carefully through resumes to develop a short list of people to interview. Try to interview at least three people and no more than five (another glimpse of how this mimics a client's selection process of shortlisting). Too many candidates make comparisons increasingly difficult and lengthens the interview process, exhausting your committees.

A prepared list of questions is important to keep the conversation on-track, to elicit responses on important topics, and to maintain a level playing field for all the candidates that will allow easier comparisons. Ask questions that reveal key attributes. Provide these questions on a scoring sheet to your interview panel to allow them to take notes on each candidate. The consistency with which you interview candidates will set up an apples-to-apples comparison at the end of the process.

In our mind, the most important sign you're looking for during the interview is "attitude." For a technical business developer, their past performance at another firm will be a key element of the discussion. Their current client base, project opportunities, and markets will also be important. But the subtext of the conversation will be attempting to obtain a sense of the attributes they carry. Call their references; do they use any of the words described earlier?

> *Talking about hiring staff brings to mind our own employment. The most important events in our careers, understandably, have been those related to getting hired (as well as getting, as we call it, de-hired). These experiences bring us full circle to the qualities that business developers and marketers should strive for and that hiring managers should look for. The single most important driver that all employees should keep in mind is **provide visible value**. Prove that you deserve your job every day.*

For marketing staff, the same applies. Marketers who are hoping to be elevated to a position in which they no longer have to be involved in proposals are to be avoided. Too often, marketers are hoping to be placed into positions in which they feel they no longer need to engage in pursuits, but rather only to "direct traffic." That is a marketer who no longer understands the meaning of the role. Likewise for business developers and those who are promoted to managers, keeping involved in proposals helps you stay sharp, no matter your position in the firm.

The interview conversation must elicit information pertaining to the attitude of the candidate toward the role. Their desire for the job can be quickly determined when they are on the job, but during an interview, when they are hungry for work and you are anxious to fill a position, it can be more challenging to ascertain. That's why you need a team of people, all looking for the right qualities, asking pertinent questions, and identifying a good fit for your firm.

Interviewing candidates is one of the most valuable learning tools for marketers and business developers because it turns the tables on the selection process. It forces you to see the process from the "clients' eyes." One of the more interesting learning aspects is discovering how challenging it is to remember all the information that is thrust on you. An hour's conversation with each of four candidates over the course of two or three days involves, even with careful notetaking, an enormous amount of information, both what the candidates say and what you think about what they say. So, remember, when you are preparing your BD team to interview for a major project, they also will be inundated with material. And when you see them not taking any notes (as many don't), then be sure to tell them exactly, in as few words as possible, why they should hire you. And make it memorable.

Some things to look for during the interview:
- Candidates who don't know the major details or monetary value of the last proposal they worked on. This shows a lack of connection between working on proposals and the resulting sales. Good marketers are results-driven and know what the bottom line is.
- Candidates who don't have any questions for you. Some candidates are just looking for a job. They don't really care what it is or for whom. You're looking for people much more engaged; people who have intense curiosity.
- Politically correct or rehearsed responses such as, "My greatest weakness is not knowing when to slow down, even when I am working my fingers to the bone."

Fourth: Decide. At the end of the interview stage, a facilitator from within the group should lead a discussion to measure the candidates and to gain consensus on a selected staff member. The job of the facilitator is to create an atmosphere in which each panel member voices their thoughts, and a decision can be made, then justified to management as a good investment for the company. It is critical that the team who will eventually work with the new person feel as if they have brought onboard a valuable complement to their team.

<u>Fifth: Negotiate.</u> After selecting the salesperson or marketer that best fits the needs of your organization, you need to bring them onboard. That can be as challenging a process as interviewing. Many of the people you want to hire are already gainfully employed. The time between telling your selected candidate that they are your top choice and their first day on the job can often feel like a game of poker, with two adversaries not wanting to show their hands. It's the opposite of how you want an effective relationship to start, but is necessary.

If trust is critical to a relationship, it is critical to a negotiation. If your candidate does not trust that you are being open about the negotiation process, they're not likely to accept an offer. Your job as employer during the negotiation process is to:

1. Protect the interests of the company by selecting candidates who will prove to be valuable long-term employees
2. Make the best investment possible of the company's limited funds
3. Introduce an employee into a team of people in a way that maintains parity, knowing that most staff can find out what their fellow employees are earning.
4. Bring to your organization game-changing people who will influence the culture of the company toward sales-oriented thinking.
5. Ensure compliance with company hiring policies and employment law.

As a potential employee, your job is to:

1. Maximize your earning potential, balancing your short-term earnings with long-term possibilities.
2. Join a company that matches your long-term career goals.
3. Understand the expectations of the firm and ask questions until you feel you know what it will take to succeed.
4. Feel confident that the people you've met will support you, trust you and appreciate your effort.

A couple of days after his initial request, your boss comes back into your office. "Where's the new hire? Did you get started yet?"

"I was just coming to your office. First, I'd like to interview you about the role you're expecting to fill. What

areas of our business plan do you want this person to be engaged in? What's the sales goal you're expecting, and how long a period of time will you allow them to get there? Then I was going to enlist you in the committee to look through the resumes, help me shortlist candidates, then interview them. I have a list of questions we will be asking the applicants. I'll be facilitating the selection process, but wanted you to be a part of this, since the selected applicant will be reporting to you."

"Wow," your boss says. "Seems like you know what you're doing."

Chapter 7
Communication and Branding

"The most important thing in communication is
To hear what isn't being said."
- Peter Drucker, Management Consultant and Professor

First scenario: you walk into the office of a potential client you have never met. You shake her hand. "Hi, I'm Charles," you say. "I work for ABC Consultants." STOP. Freeze the scene. Your prospect's arm is still extended. In order to have a successful meeting, you want her to have a positive image in her mind at that moment. You want her thinking, "I've heard good things about this firm."

Second scenario: you meet a staff member from a competing firm for lunch. He is technically brilliant and a savvy business developer. You say, "I want you to jump over to my firm." STOP. Freeze the moment. The recruit's mind is in mid-thought. He's thinking, "I like this firm. I might consider joining them."

The concept of branding and corporate communication for a professional services firm is contained in these two moments— in planting a positive image in a prospect's mind prior to meeting them to lay a solid foundation for you.

Understanding Corporate Communication

There's often a dynamic tension between the people responsible for Corporate Communication and the technical staff members of professional services firm. Some of it has to do with the normal tension between billable staff and overhead staff. Some of it can be attributed to the differences of personalities of technical professionals, or rocket scientists, versus the writers and artists that make up a communication team. Some of it might have to do with a lack of understanding or appreciation of the role of communication within the firm.

In our minds, the scenarios described at the beginning of this chapter define the mission of communications at a technical services firm: *To develop programs and collateral that effectively build favorable awareness of your firm to prospective and existing clients, employees, and partners to support your sales staff in strengthening relationships.*

There are a million activities contained in that statement, and another million things that a typical communication group is asked to perform, but the mission is straightforward. Imagine potential clients and employees saying, "Who the heck is that firm; never heard of them? Did they drop out of the sky?" You are not going to be able to make a sale or hire a recruit unless our firm becomes known to the people with whom you want to work. So, you build awareness. Let's look at the elements in more detail.

Building Awareness

The last thing you want someone to say about your firm is, "Who are they?" In order to avoid this awful tag, every firm should strive to become known in their marketplace. By speaking directly, "one-to-one", with your potential clients and teaming partners, your employees create the relationships needed to win work. You can also reach your intended contacts through activities that reach "one-to-many." Your corporate communication program is responsible for this, using such methods as:

- Brochures
- Statements of Qualifications
- Web site
- Social media
- Newsletters and mailings
- Advertising
- Technical articles and publications
- Awards programs
- Press releases
- Participation by your staff in professional organizations and attendance at conferences (covered in the next chapter).

But while these vehicles may improve your favorable awareness, they won't contribute to building interpersonal relationships. We find that many technical professionals confuse awareness with relationships. Though a firm may periodically get selected for work off the back of favorable awareness alone, it will never be enough to sustain or grow a firm.

Unless you have people in the company establishing strong relationships, and caring for them, your time will run out. This limitation frustrates those technical professionals who want to compare their firms to businesses that sell consumer products or "mass market" consumer services (such as oil changes, haircuts, or lawn care).

Obviously, if you are selling haircuts, you can mass advertise with the intention of selling your service to as many people as possible, all of whom are potential customers. Knowing the limitation and the focus of an "awareness building" program, let's look in more detail at its elements.

Brochures

Many firms invest tens of thousands of dollars into developing brochures. Business developers give them to clients, who read them and presumably say, "Gee, you seem to perform a lot of services. I'll hire you." The obvious question is: If the business developer is sitting in the room, why does it take a brochure to describe the services the firm provides? Why can't the salesperson simply tell the client what the firm can do for him or her?

The answer to that question lies in a short reminder of communication styles. To effectively persuade a person to accept your firm, you must tailor your communication to match your audience's needs. Philosophers and psychologists have grouped common behavior into four predominant styles, sometimes called Analytical, Driver, Amiable, and Expressive[5]. Some people will be persuaded after being presented with detailed data regarding your firm (Analytical). Some people want to determine on their own what information they desire to see from you (Driver). Some people are persuaded by knowing that your services have been used by other people they respect (Amiable). Still others are interested in knowing that you will listen to them and are compatible with their working style (Expressive). The job of the communication staff is to provide material that best meets the communication styles of your clients, recruits, and employees. Therefore, we feel that a brochure can be useful to those clients who feel most comfortable with having data regarding your firm that they can peruse at their leisure (Analyticals). Brochures will also be useful only if they contain information that is pertinent to the Driver. And we also understand that your expensive brochures will end up in the garbage cans of Amiables and Expressives, as soon as you leave the room. It's not the fault of the brochures; they simply do not meet the communication needs of that type of person. Those people would rather talk with you. By nature, then, brochures will be hit or miss. So, an effective program should include some investment in brochures, but they should only be one element in your overall arsenal.

Regarding brochures, there's also an element of "comparison" at play. A firm that produces a first-class brochure can be seen as being at the "same level" as other firms with those capabilities. So, a five person firm can, in some ways, be compared to a 5,000 person firm— on paper. Likewise, a 5,000 person firm with a brochure that looks like it was printed on a laser printer can lose some prestige.

In addition, brochures are sometimes used as security blankets or surrogates for staff who are not interested in visiting clients. You sometimes hear, "Let's send a brochure to this list of 5,000 potential clients." That is translated to mean, "I don't want to visit anyone. Maybe we'll get lucky and someone will call us." Our bottom line on brochures: Make some. Make them nice. You'll be asked to make a brochure for every niche service you provide. Resist it. Make a couple that fall into categories of interest to your clients, not for every silo in the firm. Don't mail them out.

---

[5] Merrill, David W., and Roger H. Reid. Personal Styles & Effective Performance. Radnor, PA: Chilton Book, 1981

Statements of Qualifications

Similar to brochures, Statements of Qualifications describe your company in all its pride and glory. There has always been a steady demand for SOQs. They will be useful for Analytical clients who value additional information after meeting with you. Tailored documents for specific opportunities are even better. However, these can be challenging to produce because of the time required for developing a unique document. Marketing staff are typically focused on proposal deadlines, so any document that does not have a specific due date will always have a lower priority. We've also noticed a trend in which having a tailored SOQ needs to be designed at the same level as your brochures. This can be time-consuming for marketing and technical staff. An SOQ which can serve more than one client tends to be a more cost-effective investment.

Web Site

Not surprisingly, developing and maintaining a web site can be the most expensive element of your communication program. Very few of us are programmers or employ them, so we're dependent on outside vendors to develop and, more importantly, maintain our websites. It automatically puts us on the defensive.

What does a web site do? Are they a business development tool, or used for recruiting? Who goes to your web site? Those are the fundamental questions to ask of your internet presence. Many sites began life as an expensive electronic version of your brochure. But over time, they have developed into useful tools for people interested in learning more about your firm. With the advent of web sites linked to social networks, a newfound potential to extend your firm's reach has been discovered that is limited only by imagination.

Aiming for Clients

It's simple to say to a client, "If you want to know more about our firm, visit our website." That would avoid all the cost of developing brochures that are outdated the moment they're printed. Would a client take the time to visit your site? It seems a lot to ask. So you might think about adding something of value that would make a visit to your site a worthwhile investment of time for your clients. Perhaps links to new regulations or white papers regarding new technologies. Those are value-added items that would increase the possibility of a client visiting your web site. The strategy involves, 1) organizing a web site that creates an easy path for your clients to find those interesting links, and 2) training your business developers to communicate to your clients that this information exists–and to hype it. Many sites we've visited carry out the first part relatively well. It's the second part that usually falls short.

We often fail to train our sales staff to sell the value of the web site's information. You shouldn't follow the adage, "Build it, and they will come." Rather, they should think, "Build it and sell it." An internal sales program can show and sell your client-facing staff this new arrow for their quiver.

Aiming at Recruits

Most analyses of web sites tell us that the predominant traffic to a technical services firm's web site is from potential employees who want to check out your company. The web site's value is significant as a recruiting tool. College students, unfulfilled professionals, and unemployed staff are coming to your web site to see where your offices are, how many people you employ, what services you offer, and to fill out a job application.

That's a great thing. There's a huge benefit to a site that attracts people to apply for a position at your firm. So, your communication staff should be partnered with your human resources department to view the web site through the lens of a recruiter. Make basic information easy to find. Put the Employment Application within two clicks of the Home Page. Keep an up-to-date list of job openings on your site. Again, as with the client information pages, make the information easy to find.

Obviously, the web site is a source of advertising for your firm. It's a great place for general corporate information, highlighting key services, and posting news releases. You can also provide helpful coordinates for access to your corporate office and branch locations. If your firm is publicly traded, many required documents to shareholders, banks, and the media can conveniently be stored and accessed here, as well.

Make no mistake, developing a decent web site is expensive. Almost no one creates a site in-house. The most common scenario is a team of 50-year old execs sitting around a table with a 24-year old web programmer, while everyone talks at cross purposes.

Developing a web site is similar to organizing the company picnic—there's need for diverse viewpoints, and it's very political. Select a great organizer to run the program and make sure to include a cross section of the company—marketing, HR, client managers, technical specialists, and recruiting. Set a budget, but beware that most web site production budgets are like home remodeling budgets, a desperate attempt to control costs in the best of circumstances. The programmer is challenged to describe how much it will cost. Your boss is trying to put a damper on your wish list. For the most part, you have to suck it up and pay to get it up and running.

We have found that a web site development project tends to be under the control of established corporate groups led by senior people. However, keep in mind that the newer generation of technical professionals has very different views of media. Our recommendation is to engage junior staff to provide input and direction, perhaps even to cede some control of content to them; you may be pleased with the results.

Updating the Web Site

The obvious difference between a brochure and a web site is that it is dynamic and needs constant updating. That's no small part of the program. We're talking about the continuous creation of content until the end of time. That type of attention is the most difficult challenge of any firm because they don't ordinarily have staff that can make the web site a priority. Marketing staff are too busy focusing on the next deadline. Graphic designers or technical writers, which some firms employ full-time, most often don't have the web skills or the ability to create content. And we find that, while engineers/scientists are continually advocating for updates, they procrastinate after committing to produce meaningful content.

So, it's a challenge across our industry. Visit any of your competitors' websites and you'll see year-old press releases, staff no longer with the firm, and pictures of projects in construction that have been operating for years. If that's the case with your firm, then you've purchased an expensive, stale electronic brochure. This is ironic because the true value of a web site is the fact that it can be dynamically updated. As in a daily newspaper, there are the basic elements that don't change, such as the masthead, the placement of sections, the background. But within that structure, there are opportunities to provide up-to-the-minute information to people. Almost no firm takes advantage of this, because they do not have the time. In addition, an average employee may jump on the internet a dozen times a day to search for information, but probably will only visit their own firm's website once a year. So, it's out of sight, out of mind.

Here's another point: if all it took to win work was a current web site, more time and energy would be invested by all of us. Because there is no causal link between updated content and signed backlog for technical services firms, the chore sits on the back burner. Another way of putting this is that we haven't heard a client say they awarded a contract to us because of an up-to-date web site.

The perfect website is one that is useful to clients, prospects, potential employees, current employees, the media, and anyone else searching for information. If the site shifts too heavily in one direction (for example, listing job openings as its primary function), then it loses its potential to be a crossroads for people who share interest in your firm.

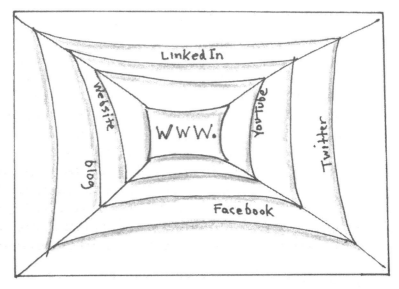

There's no simple answer to keeping a site updated. But the most likely solution is to make it a shared responsibility among marketing (to provide information on recent wins), communication (to provide recent press-worthy news), technical staff (to provide information useful to clients), human resources (to solicit new recruits), and leadership (to send a message to staff and clients on the value they place on communication).

Social Media

An interesting phenomenon related to your on-line presence is the development of social networking sites. Facebook, YouTube, LinkedIn, and Twitter have transformed the landscape for web-based communication. Typical to many phenomena, the origins of social networking started on college campuses. And typical to many phenomena, technical professional services firms have been among the last to take advantage.

First, what's the point of social networking? Certainly, networking among staff in varied locations is a great thing. And so is networking between staff and clients. But the roots of these systems are social (extremely social). Connecting business development into this activity is very tricky.

Because of the social nature of Facebook, the on-line community is very sensitive to anyone trying to "sell" something. So, advertising your firm's services is often met with derision. Who would you solicit anyway? The Facebook pages of businesses can be informative, and certainly are easier to keep up-to-date, a challenge for most websites.

The value of social media for technical services firms is in the very nature of these technologies—for individuals to stay connected with individuals. Our advice, get your project managers and business developers to connect with their clients, get your marketers to connect with other marketers, your CFO with other CFOs... you get the picture. The technology is a gift for people to stay connected, but who are challenged with making the number of phone calls necessary to build a relationship.

The interconnectedness of social media sites and your web page allows each access point to support the other. If your Facebook page drives people to your web site, and your Linked-In profile connects to your Twitter account, then each site can provide complementary information, based on the strength of each site— Twitter for speed, You Tube for video, Facebook for multimedia, Linked-in for relationships, and your web for details.

Newsletters and Mailings

The real question is, "how much information do you want your clients to receive that does not come from the mouths of your staff?" Face it, people get enough mail. They don't need any more. And no one ever selected a technical services firm based on the quality of the mailer they received. View these vehicles as a client "touchpoint," and nothing more.

While there is a need to understand and accommodate the communication styles of our clients, there is no style that demands an extra piece of mail every month. When you hire a staff member, introduce him/her to your clients; when you win an award for a technically interesting project, tell your clients. Is that inefficient? Sure. Relationship-based services are by their very nature a costly and time consuming industry to develop new business. Selling a two-dollar Chia Pet® for twenty dollars to 10,000 people for the cost of a television ad is much more efficient marketing, but, sigh, it won't work for us! You must take care to never lose sight of the inherent nature of our industry. Though many ideas from the marketing of consumer products can be useful, replacing one-on-one relationships is not among them.

Newsletters come in all shapes and sizes, and can cover company news and internal employee events. We have seen well-conceived topical newsletters, which cover such items as technology trends or regulatory updates. We have also seen internally-focused employee news sent to clients, and this always seems odd, because of the informal nature of the writing. Although you're not likely to offend a client who is reading the employee newsletter, it's hard to imagine impressing a client. Do they really want to know who had a baby this week?

Advertising

One of those aspects of consumer product marketing that has moved into the services industry is media advertising. Most of the effective opportunities to advertise your firm are within the pages of the publications produced by the professional associations with whom you are members. Though the readership is heavily weighted toward competitors (as opposed to clients), some firms find value in building name recognition among potential recruits who work at peer firms.

From a business development standpoint, advertising in trade association publications adds no value to sales unless potential clients are readers. Therefore, it is important to pay attention to what your clients are reading. Client visits should include noticing the magazines on the coffee table in the lobby. Even if your clients reads the publications in which you advertise, what do you expect them to think or do? Perhaps, if your ad is adjacent to a larger competitor, you may be viewed as a "player" by association. No client will say that they hired a firm because they spied your logo in the local trade journal, however, a subliminal connection between the client seeing an ad, then recognizing the name of your firm upon receiving a call from your business developer, may help secure a meeting.

We would also offer that technical services firms are often solicited to pay for advertising, often in the form of "business cards" placed in the back of some periodicals. Clients frequently make these requests, and the value of contributing is returned as good will. The advertising value itself is negligible, but the appreciation of a client looking to defray the cost of a publication for their professional society can be worthwhile.

Technical Articles and Publications

In addition to advertising in journals or other publications, technical services firms also publish articles to communicate to clients. Similar to many areas of academia, the majority of publications in the technical services industry are populated by articles written by the readers themselves. As described in our Chapter on Effective Trade Show and Conference Attendance, the academic model of peer review and acceptance through publication is a healthy part of the industry. Again, from a business development perspective, if your clients are reading the articles, they are likely to develop a positive perception of your abilities.

Sometimes, firms reprint their most interesting articles and send them directly to clients. This doubles up on the use of the article, which leverages the cost of writing it, but our opinion is, "if a client is interested in reading about your staff's great ideas, just think how impressed they would be if they heard about it directly from you (face-to-face)."

Articles can be time consuming to write, and the cost of writing them is often borne by your business development budget. Many firms ask that staff contribute a portion of their own time when authoring articles, and in return offer an honorarium or stipend as a modest reward.

Two additional points about technical articles: first, many professionals serve on committees as peer reviewers for technical articles. Clients who frequently chair these governing bodies are appreciative. We view the opportunity to rub shoulders with these clients as a residual

We find many technical professionals who over-value awards programs. Naturally, most technical professionals appreciate the recognition of their peers for hard work and successful projects. But there is a limit to its cost-benefit.

Keep in mind that like everything else, costs have escalated. This applies to the time and money required to assemble a winning award application. There are talented consultants who specialize in this, and we recommend you consider this as an alternative to doing these in-house. Nonetheless, the costs of doing more than a few of these can accumulate, especially if your firm is performing all of the heavy lifting without much help from your client.

We recommend you be strategic about your nominations. Look for your best clients, or the most deserving staff. Or identify a project for which the awareness of an award will catapult your firm to a new service or new geography. You'll get the most mileage out of your investment, and improve both internal and external relationships at the same time.

benefit. Some would argue this isn't even a residual benefit, rather a way to get closer to clients who won't meet with you in their own office. Second, committee work of this type also offers a valuable window into innovative and cutting edge developments.

Awards Programs

Engineers, architects, and other technical professionals love to give themselves awards. As a result, we have eaten many rubber chickens at awards ceremonies. We also have seen many crystal, silver, and gold awards on reception desks across the country, honoring impressive accomplishments. Similar to journal articles, awards are indirect evidence of technical skill to potential clients.

More so, awards programs are a great way to stay connected to your clients. Integrating them into the process is an important factor. The award, after all, is really for them. There's no better feeling than sitting at a banquet table with your client, hearing that your project has been selected for an award, and walking together to the podium to accept it.

Too often, firms internalize the program and make it all about themselves. Your technical teams are to be celebrated, awarded, and lauded, no doubt. But if the client is not involved in the program, you are missing the point, and you're not teaching your staff the fundamental importance of the client's involvement in everything you do. Measure your investment in these activities, ask your clients to be your partner, and balance the effort with the value it brings to sales.

Press Releases

Many firms produce press releases at a voluminous pace. The typical subjects are announcements of new hires, promotions, professional awards, office openings and relocations, new service offerings, and key contract awards. The questions you must ask about your press releases are the same as the one you ask regarding all of your publications, "who's reading them?" In addition, more recently you might sadly ask, "are there any publications left who will print them?" You certainly should be making announcements to clients and potential recruits regarding the activities of your company. We feel, more than anything, these announcements should go to your client managers as "talking points" for their face-to-face meetings with clients.

The best guidance we can offer is to make press releases as memorable as possible. Announcements of new hires should be accompanied by professional portrait photographs. Also, introducing a new service or offering should be accompanied by an explanation of why the client should care. Don't take for granted that the need for a new service or technology is obvious. You probably have less than three sentences or bullets to get your message across before the announcement is flung into the circular file. Consider delivering all of your announcements by e-mail. Proponents of sustainability like this approach because it avoids waste of material. The same rules apply to the electronic world; too many e-mails are likely to be regarded as spam.

In summary, it goes without saying that you should know your best clients like you know your mother-in-law. You should know their favorite restaurant, which newspaper they read, the magazines on their coffee tables, the names of their friends. Connecting their reading habits to your advertising, article writing, press releases, and other indirect marketing is the most critical part of your communication program.

Branding

Imagine you and a competitor are both trying to get a meeting with a prospective client whom neither of you had ever met. When you call, the client asks you several probing questions, but then puts you off. Yet, when your competitor calls, the client agrees to a meeting. You might have been the victim of a superior brand. If you were to crawl inside the mind of the prospective client, she might have been thinking, "I didn't know either of these guys, but I've heard positive things about one of the firms."

Competing against a firm whose positive reputation provides an entrée to clients places you at a disadvantage. You find that you're introducing your firm to everyone you meet, one at a time, while everyone seems to have heard of the other firm. Your competitor has a healthy head start over you in this situation.

Your brand is one your firm's most valuable assets. A brand is created by the experiences people have with you, or the experiences they've heard about. These experiences create perceptions, which people carry with them, share with others, and remember until the next time you meet. Your brand is like a name tag that gives people information on who you are, before you've introduced yourself. It might say, "Hello, I'm from Company x. We're low cost." Or perhaps, "I'm with Company y. We're fun to work with." Identifying and developing the right phrase for that name tag is the art behind the complex task of branding your technical firm.

To gain a clear under-standing of the power of brand-ing, you must first shift your viewpoint from where it typi-cally resides-- inside yourself-- to an outside perspective. Without sounding too Zen, we are simply describing the ne-cessity for self-awareness as a critical factor in "formulating and managing" your brand. For some firms, engaging with the topic of branding is a journey of enlightenment; for others, it's a death march because of the resistance put up by rocket scientists. This is what we know:

The Art of Developing Your Brand

The first necessity of branding is to be convinced that the leaders of your firm believe that it is relevant to a technical services firm and that it can be applied to meet stra-tegic goals. Most service-based firms assume that they have little in common with consum-er product-based companies for whom brand awareness is eve-rything. The value of the branding to soda companies is obvious. While caramel-colored, carbonated sugar wa-

*We find a lot of interpretation be-ing applied to the definition of a brand. It's important to grasp several associated concepts, in order to appreciate the meaning to your firm. We like the sim-plistic explanation offered by Wikipedia: "Brand is the image of the product in the market. The experiential aspect consists of the sum of all points of contact with the brand and is known as the **brand experience**. The psychological aspect, sometimes referred to as the **brand im-age**, is a symbolic construct created within the minds of people and consists of all the information and expectations associated with a product or service." ("Brand." Wikipedia. Wikimedia Founda-tion, 22 Apr. 2014. Web.)*

The act of branding a technical ser-vices firm differs from that of branding a product, or even consumer services. This is because of both the complexity and highly personal nature of these services. You might be willing to have your oil changed by any mechanic, but it's unlike-ly that you would select a project manag-er you've never met before to design your nuclear power plant.

*We also would point out from our experience that many scientists and en-gineers find discussions of branding to be elusive. This is understandable because it deals with human emotion and is highly subjective. Be on the lookout for conver-sations devolving into a debate over trademarks or logos. While these may be important to advertising, they represent only a slice of the tools for achieving **brand identity**.*

ter is their product, the rabid allegiance of their customers is a result of masterful branding. In fact, developing a *brand relationship* of this nature is the holy grail for consumer product marketers, and increasingly so for those who offer technical services.

The art of selling technical services revolves around convincing cli-

ents to select you for an assignment. And persuasion is about differentiating your firm from all others. But you can't discover those differentiators unless you have a keen understanding of how your firm is perceived by your clients.

Branding is so critical to your sales effort and to recruiting and retaining talented employees that your CEO should "own" it, and that it should have buy-in from all quarters of the firm. Not a small task. The reason most technical services firms don't engage with the concept of branding is because: 1) they don't see the connection between branding and an increase in sales, 2) they're too busy, or 3) they don't know where to start.

We strongly recommend that the marketing organization lead this effort because of the profound impact on sales, and its strong connectivity to clients. Volunteering to lead the development of your firm's brand is a high-value use of time and it can be approached in a practical manner.

Organizing a Branding Campaign

A critical initial step is to listen to your clients and staff members. The stories they tell about your firm are the foundation of your effort. Ask them pointed questions about their perception of who your company is, what it does, why it's different, and why it matters. The "nature" of a company is not about rebar and concrete, spreadsheets, or lines of computer code; instead, it's about the reason clients choose to work with you. They select you over your competition because of the way you work with them and the cumulative experiences they derive.

Achieve a balanced range of perspectives when obtaining input from employees. Long-time employees provide a valuable historical reference, but can also be myopic and territorial. New employees are an important source of information for external perceptions because they have recently been on the outside. Both groups are resources that can provide valuable comparisons.

Differentiators are the unique descriptors of your organization. You can talk about your company all you want, but unless you explore the differences between you and your competitors, then all you'll be producing is a documentary-like description of your firm's legacy. What you're aiming for is the difference between a photograph of the seaside and an Impressionist painting of the seaside—an original perspective and interpretation that is instantly recognizable. The next step is to look at all this language and find common elements. These common themes form the core elements of your brand.

Questions for client interviews:

1. Debrief of last selection of the firm. Why did you select us? What made us stand out from the other firms?

2. What do you look for in a consultant, in general?

3. What has disappointed you about a firm in the past?

4. What are your greatest challenges as an organization?

Questions for new employee interviews:

1. What were the major reasons you joined our firm?

2. Is the firm different than you expected?

3. What impresses you most about the firm?

4. What disappoints you?

You may find that there are some elements of your firm's nature that you don't want to encourage. For example, the consensus of the groups you speak with could lead you to think that "old-fashioned" is a particular characteristic of your firm. While it may be a common perception, it is clearly not a nature that benefits clients, nor draws new employees to you. So, even though you have teased out an important personality trait of your firm, it's not part of your brand, unless it can be utilized to advance your strategic plan.

Separating the Words From the Pictures

We're sure you've noticed that we have not yet discussed what many believe to be a critical component to branding—logos and colors. Your visual identity is a powerful component of your brand. Identifiable icons, such as Apple's apple and Nike's swoosh, are billion dollar assets. When your company literally owns a color the way Tiffany owns light blue, then you've achieved a powerful differentiator.

But at the beginning of your branding process, it's imperative that you first capture the language that describes your firm. At the challenging point of the process, during which you are compressing the definition of your firm into a few memorable words, you need to remain focused. It's too easy to let yourself off the hook and believe that a visually striking logo will make up for an unfocused brand message.

We recommend that you clearly separate the process of brand messaging and visual identity. Develop your message, declare success, then move into a graphic development phase that utilizes all you have developed.

Overwhelmed with Language

At the end of your initial meetings, you'll have developed a great deal of written material; stories, narratives, word combinations, impressions, as well as specific descriptions of how your firm is perceived.

An obvious next step is to look through your material and attempt to spot connections and repetition. You'll hopefully see that the universe of words you have developed will coalesce into galaxies of similar themes. For example, phrases such as "our firm encourages innovative thinkers" and "our firm is noted for its strong-minded staff" and "we are privately-owned" may seem to gravitate toward a theme that might be titled "Independent." These themes are elements of your firm's nature that resonate with people and their experiences with you.

How do you know if the words you're connecting to your firm are really your brand? The descriptors that you select as your brand need to be useful, which can include: advancing your strategic plan goals, being beneficial to clients, or being attractive to employees. If the words you select don't meet these criteria, then you've only succeeded in describing your firm, not branding it. The brand language has to specifically be connected with the mercenary tasks of winning new work, and attracting and retaining talent to the firm.

For example, you can say that your firm is "innovative." Testing it, the word certainly advances your goals and is memorable; it might differentiate you (if you truly thought no other firm in your category was innovative, which we doubt). But exactly how does innovation benefit your clients? Many clients (based on the client interviews you performed) might be telling you that they don't want to pay for your company to perform cutting-edge research. But perhaps new recruits are telling you that the company's reputation as technology leaders was attractive to them. You have to overcome the "so what?" factor of your clients. What part of your firm's nature of innovation benefits them? Perhaps: "the firm's technology and process innovations lead to practical and cost-effective solutions for clients." The "trigger," a memorable word or phrase that elicits a memory of those crystalline sentences, could be named, "practical innovation." This is the type of connecting, testing, naming, and compressing that challenges your staff to think from their client's perspective and get to the heart of the company's core relevancy in the marketplace.

Brand Implementation

The nagging question that stays with us regarding the branding process is, "Once you have brand, what do you do with it?" You finally get to a point at which you've fiddled enough with the language, and you've crafted the messages that eloquently differentiate your firm. How do you release it to your organization and to your clients?

Successfully implementing a brand requires persuading everyone in your firm to align around a common idea-- an idea that the work the firm does is transformative. That idea is what draws clients and future employees to you. All employees are interested in working with a company that is separated from its competitors and that wins work consistently. Who wouldn't? For Apple, Coke or Samsung, hundreds of millions of dollars in advertising and industrial design are directed toward creating perceived differentiators in the minds of customers. To us in technical services firms, we have to convince people literally one-by-one, since personal relationships are the core of our service.

The first step in introducing a formal brand into your service organization is to teach your staff the language. Just as you would teach someone a foreign language, you wouldn't throw a primer at them and say, "Learn this and let me know when you're fluent." Foreign language education involves a methodical approach of introducing vocabulary, parts of speech, and useful phrases through a process of immersion. A brand can be a foreign concept to your staff; you should introduce it slowly to assure that everyone is learning at the same pace.

The first concept to teach your staff is the definition of branding, as it relates to a professional services firm. You may find that the word "branding" carries negative connotations, as if it cheapens the importance of your technical service. You aren't, after all, a box of breakfast cereal. Take the argument off the table and call your program an "identity plan" or a "reputation management plan."

Your brand messages are the first phrases that you teach. Your short memorable "triggers" should become ingrained in your staff's consciousness in the same way you teach someone the French language, through repetition. Though your brand message is easy to memorize, it needs to become second nature to your staff. Imprint it on coffee mugs, water bottles, shirts, thumb drives, any place you can display it. Use coordinated tactics such as piggybacking your brand messages onto your traditional communication tools: perhaps your in-house newsletter, your intranet site, or in the signature block at the bottom of e-mail. Get the messages out there.

Next, find gathering places of people in the company to introduce your brand. Find a marketing meeting, a new staff orientation, an office party, or training session. In this manner, you develop your Brand Champions, who can carry the ideas forward.

Brand Champions

Once your employees understand the elements of your firm that make it unique, they can communicate them to clients. A solid brand simplifies communication and action throughout the firm by providing a way to prioritize how you act and what you say. It's a roadmap to guide everyone in your company toward consistently positive interactions with clients and one another. If your brand message is based on your *responsiveness to clients*, then you hire receptionists who are quick on their feet, purchase a voicemail system that is state-of-the-art, prepare a communication policy that encourages returning phone calls the same day. Not only do you have marching orders on how to communicate at the office, but every time someone answers their messages promptly, you've reinforced your brand and made it stronger. This continuous "do-loop" of consistent action and interaction creates the type of momentum that defines strong brands.

> *You meet a staff member from a competing firm for lunch. He is technically brilliant and a savvy business developer. You think he would be a good addition to the firm. You tell him, "I want you to jump over to my firm." STOP. Freeze the moment. The recruit's mind is in mid-thought. He's thinking about everything that he has ever heard about your firm. He remembers what clients have said about you. He thinks about the mailings he has received and the e-mail announcements. He thinks to himself, "I know this firm. I like them. I might consider joining them." That's an effective use of a brand.*

Chapter 8
Effective Conference and
Trade Show Attendance

"It's better to look good than to feel good."
- Billy Crystal, as Ricardo Montelbaum.

You're at the annual conference of the Association of Financial Advisors in Walla Walla, Washington. It's Friday night. You stand at the threshold of an enormous banquet hall. 600 attendees search for seats.

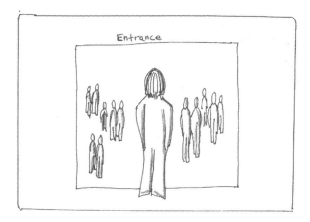

The program for the evening includes speeches by the officers of the association, then a talented hypnotist will lull people to sleep and coax several of them to cluck like chickens. The menu consists of overcooked steak, dry potatoes, and sugar-bomb cake.

As you walk between the tables, your choice of seating is the table of strangers at your left or the table of strangers at your right. You feel your throat dry up; you stuff your hands deep inside your pockets.

You think, "What am I doing here? How could this possibly be contributing to our company's sales?"

There are many activities a firm can perform to ease the path for business developers before they meet with a client. A rock solid communication program is one; any salesperson is thankful for useful collateral, such as brochures and SOQs. They would also appreciate the client receiving a couple of items in the mail prior to a meeting, so they would at least have some familiarity with the services the firm provided. It sure would save time in explaining who you are and why you're standing in the client's office. This was discussed in the previous chapter.

What if potential clients were already familiar with you and your firm's services from having listened to a technical presentation at a conference? That would be useful. And what about finding a way to meet with multiple clients at once? Or, the possibility of dozens or hundreds of clients hearing of your latest technical solution?

By its nature, technical services is... well, technical. The industry, like the sciences, advances the state of knowledge through peer review and sharing at conferences and symposia. Conferences also offer opportunities that combine peer review, education and business development.

Balancing Cost with Benefit

While almost every firm takes advantage of conferences and trade shows, few ask themselves, "how much will it cost, and is it worth it?" What should you expect to receive from attending a technical conference? Certainly, a technical services professional will gain knowledge; new ideas are the basis for innovating the services your firm offers to clients.

In addition, depending on the level of interaction with other people attending the conference, you can also reasonably expect to obtain such things as introductions to potential clients you have never met; deepened relationships with clients you already know; and project leads you weren't aware of. Those certainly have a monetary value.

But you say to yourself, couldn't I obtain these benefits by visiting more clients personally? This is where you consider balance. What is the cost of visiting those clients versus seeing them at a conference? How much quality "face time" will you actually get?

One way to think about this is to consider the difference between "one-to-one" connections with people versus "one-to-many." Technical services are transactions of specialized skills which require a large investment of time interacting with clients, both for developing new business and providing services. This business model is different from consumer product businesses, which invest heavily in promoting their wares to multitudes of potential buyers, expecting that they will never meet or interact with any of them.

GENERAL PERCEPTION
INDUSTRY SUPPORT
PROSPECTS
UNDERSTANDING
INTRODUCTIONS
RELATIONSHIPS
LEADS
IDEAS

Conferences

So, when making decisions regarding large venues, such as conferences and trade shows, the technical services firm should keep in mind their business model, before they invest heavily in product-style "trolling" at these events. Having said that, there are a number of valuable professional opportunities at conferences and trade shows, if properly implemented and balanced.

How much to invest

One of the first things to discuss, when building a conference attendance program, is how much to invest. What should a firm pay to "advertise" their firm's services by:

- Presenting technical papers.
- Attending conferences for the purposes of marketing (not related to professional education), including registration, travel, meals.
- Sponsorship.
- Membership on committees (these are the engines of most professional associations)?

As discussed in the chapter on "The Cost of Business Development," these activities fall under the category of Indirect Sales, which is a (hopefully) small percentage of your business development budget, compared to Direct Sales. Conferences or trade show activities should be a apportioned and budgeted as part of the overall Indirect Sales activities, which also might include brochures, websites, and other collateral.

For budgeting purposes, use the 80-20 rule to divide the labor budget and expense budget (travel, registration, meals, client dinners). Depending on the number of people attending and length of conference, your budget expands or contracts. Sounds simple, doesn't it? But trust us, you and your staff will invent the most impressive arguments on the importance of a week-long conference in Switzerland, or why two dozen of your staff need to be in Walla Walla to "provide an overwhelming show of force to frighten your competition." Just try being a gatekeeper for the budget when receiving requests for $500 ice sculptures at a hospitality suite. Let your CFO be the bad guy. "Sorry Bill, the CFO only gave us a budget of $3,000. We're out of money. I guess you can't go to Chamonix for that ski-in conference."

Not everyone can make effective use of attending a conference. You have to consider who's best suited for the activities. It's not rocket science, but we have seen many people attend a week-long event, mingle with a thousand potential prospects, and return with nothing to show for it. We've also seen people attend an hour-long lunch presentation and return to the office with a new project. Your job in building an effective attendance program is to encourage people who perform and discourage people who do not, as in all business development activities. This is doubly important for conference attendance because of the cost.

The Paths to Success at Conference and Trade Shows

There are many associations of professionals that gather on a regular basis. These organizations bring together like-minded peers with the intention of advancing the state of their industry. Some client-centric groups invite professional services firms to become "associate" members or to make presentations to its membership. The most beneficial groups are those that combine professional services firms and clients as equal members.

Professional Development

Since this is a book on marketing, we won't dwell on the topic of developing your technical skills at conferences. What we will say is that anything you learn should be shared with your fellow employees. We often see people fly off to the far reaches of the country, attend a week-long conference, then return to work with little acknowledgement that they were gone. If we were kings, we'd require every employee who attends a conference to provide a synopsis of the sessions in which they participated and to host a brown-bag lunch for their fellow employees. The cost of attending a major conference would be defrayed greatly, if the information was shared beyond just the attendee.

Technical staff members also often attend conferences without presenting a paper or participating on a panel of experts. While this is acceptable sometimes, we encourage active participation, rather than passive attendance. Full participation in the association is an opportunity to make the firm more visible in the marketplace, using "one-to-many" communication to elicit results.

Marketing

Whereas many technical professionals think that conferences are 80 percent technical opportunities and 20 percent avenues for sales, we think the opposite. Otherwise, your firm is not maximizing

As a graduate student, I was fortunate to attend a national conference of an important professional organization. Many things impressed me including the technical presentations, meeting famous researchers and professors, the exhibit hall, and free beer at hospitality suites sponsored by equipment manufacturers. I immediately knew that I wanted to attend all of these events in the future as a way to meet people and stay up to date on new technology. I was in for a rude awakening.

Within a few weeks of starting work in my new job, my graduate thesis research paper had been accepted for presentation at a national conference on the east coast. I went to book a hotel and plane tickets, and was told by my boss that new hires and junior people in general don't attend the big conferences, it was reserved for company VPs who would be there to entertain clients. He asked me if one of those VPs could present my paper.

Conferences are the ultimate crossroad of art and rocket science because of the dual emphasis on personal interaction and technical presentations and exhibits. Achieving a solid balance of technical learning and client contact can make an investment in conferences worthwhile.

Through the lobbying of a senior colleague I was able to attend the conference, present my paper, and visit a nearby water treatment plant run by someone who would eventually become a cherished client.

the investment of thousands of dollars to attend, participate, sponsor, or otherwise divert your staff away from direct sales on your home turf.

A business developer looks at a conference as an opportunity to meet one-on-one with a series of people in an efficient manner. Some conferences are in out-of-the-way locations, so you can find yourself captive in close proximity to clients over a several day period. This is an enticing opportunity for a business developer, IF the people with whom they are spending their time are potential clients. It's important to review the people who participate in the association. Is it predominantly other technical professionals? Do enough people attend the hosted events to allow interaction with a wide range of prospects? When reviewing the members of an association, you should think about a portfolio approach to relationships.

Targeted Clients: A healthy number of the people on the conference attendance list should be targeted clients that you already have been calling on. These are people who will see you from a different perspective, away from their office. It's another interaction you can achieve with them that solidifies an already fruitful relationship.

The sweet spot of those targeted clients are those who have upcoming projects for which you are positioning. A conference or association event is a place where people socialize and let their hair down (yes, sometimes drink a little too much). You can learn more about an upcoming project over a glass of wine with a client at a hospitality suite than at any pre-proposal meeting, that's certain. There's no better justification for spending BD money on a trip to a conference in Las Vegas than by using it to meet with a potential client about a project over a glass of wine. Sharing two glasses of wine? The proposal will write itself because you've been able to listen to their needs.

The next people that you should attempt to meet are clusters of targeted clients that would otherwise take a significant amount of time to meet with individually. If your targeted clients include the Public Works Directors of cities throughout Southern California, then it would make sense to find an association that corrals them in one place.

Prospects: The next tier of people to identify at conferences is prospective clients you have not yet targeted. Every business development organization should bring on new clients each year. A healthy portfolio of relationships includes potential clients in close proximity to existing clients. If your clients like you, isn't it logical to think that their neighbors may like you? A conference is a great place to have your existing clients introduce you to other people they know. Even the shyest technical professional would be comfortable at some of the social events that associations host. These events are intended to put people at ease. Take advantage of them.

For any person whose blood chills at the thought of making a cold call, a conference or trade show is a great place. It fosters "warm starts," a way to meet potential clients with a safety net.

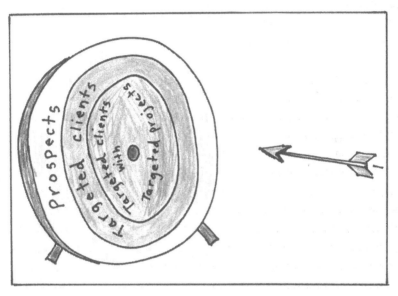

Competitors/Teaming Partners: In addition to potential clients, conferences and trade shows offer an opportunity to associate with other technical professionals. We often see that this tier of attendees – your competition—is ignored at these events. Conferences can be effective places for a business developer to assess the competitive playing field. Your competition is in the same boat—they're identifying new prospects and maintaining relationships with their clients. An observant marketer takes mental notes of everything that competitors are doing at a conference. Who are they hanging around with? What are other people saying about them? *"Keep your friends close, keep your enemies closer[6]"*— often overlooked.

---

[6] Sun Tzu, and Samuel B. Griffith. *The Art of War*. London: Oxford UP, 1971.

Every competitor is alternatively a potential teaming partner. So, building relationships with other technical professionals is an important step in the food chain. A network of relationships with people in other firms is a way to have eyes and ears in more places. Observing a rival business developer network at a conference is a way to verify the depth of relationships they claim to have. Permanent teaming partners—those technical firms that provide support services to your firm can provide not only technical support, but also relationship support. In the same manner that clients can introduce you to other potential clients, teaming partners can include you in their network.

Roving or Anchored?

One of the most frequently asked questions concerning conferences is, "Should we sponsor a booth or not?" Many trade shows provide opportunities for vendors and service providers to display their wares. This always reminds us of the county fair, where hawkers sell the newest mop or Ginzu knives. There are least two schools of thought in locating and interacting with clients at a conference. One is to register for the conference, then seek them out at technical sessions or social events. The other is to set up a booth and let them come to you. In point of fact, there is no rule to guide you, except to ENGAGE with whatever method you choose.

The problem for technical professional firms is that they don't have a product to sell.

> For a technical services firm, there's very little to be gained by standing at a trade show booth. But, it can provide an alternative to the usual menu of activities. If you're a marketer, volunteer to attend, then use the skills every successful marketer has: sociability, knowledge of your firm and, most importantly, a naturally inquisitive nature. Make every person walking by a welcome sight. Make a goal of shaking a hundred hands, gathering 30 business cards. Make the event a prospector's paradise.

They have nothing to demonstrate other than some photos of past projects velcroed to the carpeted walls of the booth, or perhaps a few statements regarding the services they provide. With nothing to demonstrate, the booth becomes essentially a "home base" for the attendees during the conference—a place for your clients to find you or for your staff to congregate. For a typical professional association, the revenue for booth sponsorships helps support the cost of the conference. A firm can gain a certain amount of gratitude from the association, though there are other sponsorship opportunities and donations that can also meet this criterion. There's also an argument that a booth provides "visibility" or name recognition. Certainly, displaying the firm's logo along a path trafficked by potential clients can't be a bad thing. Billboards have their place.

We have mixed feelings about booths at conferences. In our opinion, a booth is a crutch for staff who are uncomfortable with roaming through a conference without a tether. For aggressive salespeople, a booth is an anchor that keeps them from swimming toward their quarry. But crutches aren't bad things. They help people get around without pain.

Our advice is to make a conscious decision based on your intentions for the conference. What does the firm want to accomplish? Who will be attending? Which clients or targets do you expect to capture? If you

expect to introduce junior staff members to the conference, then having a booth gives them a place to hang their hat. If the conference has 1,000 potential client attendees, and you expect only to send three or four staff, a booth will provide some value in being seen by the many people with whom your staff can't possible interact.

There's also an argument regarding being seen as a "player." If a competitive firm has 10,000 employees and offices worldwide, while your firm has 100 employees and four offices, then if both firms host booths adjacent to each other, you can be viewed as being on the same playing field. This is interesting, but we question if clients are really convinced. So, if you can't decide, why not alternate on an annual basis between the trolling method (attending the conference and seeking out your clients) and the casting method (setting up a booth as bait). It provides variety for your staff, building their skills in both methods.

The Conference Plan

Professionals often enter an event with a singular mindset—give their paper, answer questions, then go back to the hotel. Likewise, marketing staff often think that their job is to stand at the tradeshow booth and shake hands, ignoring the opportunities to educate themselves on a topic of interest to their clients. The best mindset when entering these events is: make the maximum use of your time and the opportunities presented.

When deciding whether to attend a conference, a question to be asked is, "What does your firm want to accomplish?" Most business developers or marketers would never think of attending a meeting with a client with no preparation. Yet, many people attend conferences without reviewing the attendance list or preparing themselves for the time they will invest there. A business developer should approach a conference with the same organization as a client meeting. The considerable expense for these trips means you have to prove that the investment benefits the company.

It's a good idea to develop a plan of action. Here's one way to get organized for the event.

1. Develop a calendar of the days and evenings you'll be at the conference.

2. List the technical sessions you'd like to attend.

3. If possible, obtain a list of people who have registered for the conference. Look for people you know, as well as client organizations you've been meaning to contact. Of course, prior to the event, you should inquire of your clients whether they plan to attend.

4. Contact clients and acquaintances to set up a private breakfast or late night drink. If you schedule meetings on the periphery of the conference agenda, you won't interfere with your client's attendance at technical sessions. You may also want to organize a dinner for a group of clients. You're not the only person networking at the event; your clients are also there to meet people. They may appreciate a get-together with your other clients who share similar challenges. Put your facilitation skills to use.

> Conference Plan
> ✓ Day 1 - My intention is to talk to....
> ✓ Evening 1 - My intention is to talk to...
> ✓ Day 2 - My intention....

5. List your intentions for each day, evening, and event. Who do you want to meet? Which client do you want to connect with? How many business cards will you obtain? There's no way to assert that you achieved your goals at a conference, if you had no goals going into it.

6. If you're attending the conference with other staff members, share your calendars, so that you can divide the workload and complement each other's activities. A unified mission makes more sense than multiple people attending the same conference and being surprised when they bump into each other. "I didn't know you were coming. What are you doing here?" Not a good sign.

Elevator Speech

As discussed in the previous chapter, a major element of branding is describing yourself and your company in a consistently positive manner that maximizes the potential of connecting with people who need your services. Developing an elevator speech is a key branding tool. An elevator speech is a description of your firm, your services and differentiators that you can recite to someone you meet at a conference in the time it takes for an average elevator ride-- short and memorable. You need to arm yourself with an appealing narrative that raises the antennae of clients and makes them interested to hear more. For example, "Hi, I'm John. I'm responsible for marketing services. My firm supports American business enterprises throughout the southern states with hard-driving real estate acquisition."

Your arsenal should also include a variety of additional narratives about your company or yourself that can supplement your overall speech, adding more detail, based on inquiries from the listener. As we talk about this topic, keep in mind that many people make this up on the fly. Does that make sense? If you are attempting to differentiate yourself, you need to think through what you offer, before you trot it out in front of a hundred people at a conference.

Conferences and trade shows are exactly the type of venues that demand branded narratives. If running on all cylinders, your staff attending a major conference could talk to 100 to 1,000 people, depending on the scale of the event. Imagine the improved effectiveness if your people were on the same page when describing the services and advantages your firm provides to clients.

Follow-up

So, you've attended the conference, met some people, seen some old friends from other firms, and reacquainted yourself with several clients. You return to the office. Your e-mail inbox is full, the phone message light is blinking. You jump back into work and don't look back. Within a day you forget who you met; within two days you forget where you went; within three you forget you even left.

When you return from a conference, make a point to memorialize your activities in a short memo. You owe the firm the benefit of the investment it made. Share the technical information you learned, as well as the gossip you overheard about the state of activities at your competitors' operations.

Regarding the people you met, there's no use coming home with two dozen business cards if they lie in a stack on your desk for the rest of the year. The key to any prospecting, whether at a conference or a sales trip, is methodical, persistent follow up. Just as you developed a plan to attend the conference, you need an equally defined plan to follow up on the opportunities you uncovered.

Add upcoming project opportunities to your leads list; ask your technical specialists to follow up with answers to the questions you received that you couldn't answer. The results of a conference can be quantified, measured, and assessed. There's no doubt that you can obtain valuable information and form solid relationships at these events. Ask yourself if the people at your firm are making best use of the opportunities.

One way to determine who performs well at these events is to monitor "attendance logs." Ask attendees to submit a memo of their conference activities when they return to the office. Simply comparing activities will provide an indication of who makes effective use of their time.

In the end, conferences can be effective places for developing new business. Your program should be planned, budgeted, managed, coordinated, reported on, and measured. And it should be placed in context with the other major activities that are part of your business development program.

> *Think back to your challenge at the beginning of the chapter. It's the following year—another annual conference. This time, you're determined to make good use of your time. You walk into the banquet hall. Your plan is to find a client who has an upcoming project you're tracking. Like a laser-guided missile, you cruise through the hall until you locate him. "Bob," you say. "Good to see you again. Mind if I sit next to you?" Your client gestures you over. You introduce yourself to everyone at the table. Two of them are familiar from last year's conference.*
>
> *As the evening proceeds, you are acknowledged from the podium twice, once when you're thanked for leading a committee over the past year, and again as your firm wins an award for "Project of the Year." The client and the others at the table admire the crystal hardware.*
>
> *The chicken is still rubbery, but somehow it goes down well, knowing that you're building relationships, creating a positive impression of yourself and your firm, and laying a solid foundation for future appointments.*

Chapter 9
Marketing and Sales Systems

"Life was simple before World War II. After that, we had systems."
- R. Adm Grace Hopper, Computer Scientist and Naval Officer.

We were visiting a branch office in another state. Up at 3:30 AM to meet a 6:00 AM flight. Rental car. Map. Grande Drip. Find office. A day of marketing discussions and an all-hands lunch meeting.

We heard a lot of, "Everything's fine. No problems here." Head nods while we were talking meant, "I'm listening, but I'm not really hearing." We were looking for a way to get someone really engaged. We are asked about forms. "We thought you might want to inspect our file of completed Go/No-Go forms."

We said, "No, just take them up to the roof and throw them over the edge, thanks." That's when we finally got a reaction.

In our minds, sales are about following a methodical approach, across multiple activities, over a long period of time. It is all about systems. In addition, we find that the vast majority of technical professionals are creatures of habit. They use complex systems to run their business and, especially, to perform quality work (some of which, such as checking calculations for bridges or levees, are responsible for people's lives).

Systems can help codify best practices into routines, forcing organizations to stick to them day in, day out. As businesses grow, support systems help groups stay organized, meet deadlines, and achieve goals. We have found that many technical professionals find comfort in systems. After all, they are schooled in equations, theorems, and proofs, and adapt well to structure. If systems can be established that make sense, and genuinely help your staff get their jobs done, then you may find a surprising amount of ready acceptance.

In this chapter, we review systems, focusing on their strategic importance. A few words of caution, however. Don't become a slave to these tools. And don't lose sight of why you are doing something. The best system architects drill down to the underlying thought process, apply it as an overall guideline, and work to make the structure successful.

Systems to Track Clients, Sales, and Opportunities

Unless you belong to a one-client, one-project-at-a-time firm, most companies have developed some type of system for keeping track of clients and sales opportunities.

Client lists. This may be the simplest, but most important of all marketing systems. We haven't found a firm yet that didn't keep a list of its clients. At the very minimum, your accounting department keeps a spreadsheet, so they know where to send an invoice. It often makes sense for sales teams to build upon that central repository of information-- client name, contact name, address, and phone number. This information will be the backbone for nearly every other sales tracking system.

Perhaps you also classify clients (e.g., by service provided to them, type of business they are engaged in), so that you can plan your future actions and positioning for them. Client lists can also be divided by geography and sector, or according to however your firm is organized. This will help focus conversations on relevant services or responsibilities.

It is also important to keep a list of clients for whom you're not currently working. Accounting probably doesn't maintain that information, unless it's dormant clients with whom you have not worked in a while. As a result, it will be up to the sales and marketing staff to focus on a list of *target* clients, and to ensure that it is discussed in combination with the list of existing clients. And, no, neither the phone book nor the atlas can be considered a client list. By its nature, a list of clients and prospects is focused and vetted, even if your firm has 100,000 employees.

Contact lists. As an added dimension to a list of organizations, a catalog of the people you talk to is crucial. This list should name the individuals to whom you plan to sell your services. Basic information on these people should include coordinates for contacting them, but might also track details such as associations to which they belong, previous positions, or even names of spouses or significant others. One of the easiest ways to obtain work with a new customer is when a past client joins them, allowing you to ride on their coattails. Keeping track of people, as they move from one organization to another during their career, should be a top priority.

Offshoots of the contact list are "mailing lists" maintained for sending company newsletters, announcements, and invitations. For maximum efficiency, this should be centralized. You would be surprised by how many firms maintain separate lists of the same people—one for accounting, one for marketing, one for the project team. However, we caution that the client list should be reasonably secured; it is of enormous value to your operation, so should be guarded.

Obviously, this should go without saying (but it has come up), that you should not cross a client off your list just because you have not worked for them for a period of time. Many firms have a tendency to lose touch with old friends – don't be one of those companies.

We also add non-clients to the list of contacts, such as specialty firms, teaming partners, and other business associates who work with your company to complete projects. Or they may be prominent trade or regulatory officials who are important industry contacts. If these individuals can potentially help bring in business, they should be included as contacts.

Contact reports. In our second book, we outline the importance of written reports from client meetings. Because most major pursuits require a team effort, tracking and communicating multiple contacts by a variety of people becomes essential for coordination. These reports can be set up as a schedule of planned meetings with clients, along with details of conversations. Your marketing meetings will gain tremendous value if you systematically review status of contacts, action items, and results. This is the essence of building in accountability to your sales program. In our recent experience, most systems for this activity have a common denominator: e-mail routing. This is an effective way to distribute time-sensitive material, though storage and retrieval can be challenging unless you keep every e-mail message you've ever received or sent.

Establishing a central repository of client contact reports and important attachments offers many benefits. Many firms are adopting software for collaboration and sharing of client meeting details. These products add a layer of organization with features for updates that can be efficiently tracked by an administrator. The software also can enable the use of wikis or blogs, if appropriate. A layer of security restrictions can be added for securing sensitive information.

Customer Relationship Management (CRM). Client Relationship Management (CRM) programs are the next level of sophistication for organizing client contact data. Increasingly, we find even small firms adopting sophisticated information technology tools to support their sales and client service activities. A number of commercially available packages allow tracking of client information and results. These systems support the overall process of managing client interactions by providing proactive scheduling of actions and meetings.

Much of the discussion on the merits of these types of systems is centered around a firm taking a comprehensive and all-inclusive approach to client service. As many of us have learned, the best information technology systems in the world will not achieve their advertised benefits unless the users universally adopt the new approach. This is a big topic within information technology circles.

Sales opportunities/leads. If you track interaction with clients, it makes sense to track the sales opportunities that are developed from your client contacts. This list is also called a "sales pipeline" or "funnel." In our experience, this is one of the most important marketing systems that a firm owns. It is also one of the only "forward-looking" systems that a technical services firm possesses, as it offers a view of the future. Management can often be found attempting to predict future earnings, based on past performance. Your marketing pipeline is a better crystal ball into the financial health of the company.

In some firms, the marketing pipeline feeds a revenue forecasting process, which in turn is used by management to anticipate staffing and capital resource needs. Hence, the importance of a robust sales opportunity list, with high quality, accurate information. We recommend that the sales pipeline be linked with your proposal log (sales documents that are going out the door), since they are tracking the same information (the opportunities you are pursuing, have pursued, and are going to pursue). Don't make the mistake of carrying multiple sets of the same information – they won't reconcile, and inaccuracy creates loss of confidence in the information. Any good database software can permit sorting and subdividing by department, geography, sector, or other grouping. Included in this information should be the best estimate of potential fee, start date for the work, and probability of success. Thus, the data can provide a rudimentary projection of future revenues for the company. In addition, by inspecting the list of leads from 35,000 ft, you gain a realistic view of the size of the markets you have entered.

Lead service subscriptions. If you stay around sales long enough, you'll be approached by someone offering subscription to a lead service.

They provide regular e-mail messages of potential project opportunities, based on phone calls they've made. We confess to having used these in the past, but we are not big fans. They do have some value if they point out an opportunity you were not aware of with enough advance notice to become positioned. However, those leads are few and far between, and you must keep in mind that every other subscriber to the lead service is also reading the same information, so you will be pursuing the opportunity with all your competitors. We prefer to ask our Managers to be well-traveled, see a lot of clients, and dig up leads the old fashioned way.

Systems to Manage Pursuits and Proposal Development

Systems for supporting individual pursuits will help to manage their development.

Go/No Go Decision Support. It's unrealistic to think that every identified opportunity should be pursued. As discussed in our chapter on the Money Side of BD, the cost to pursue competitive work, from positioning through negotiations, can be enormously expensive. Therefore, a firm must be prudent in selecting the projects in which to invest. A system for supporting the decision-making process for project opportunities is an important tool.

Most business development teams ask themselves a series of questions when considering a project. These questions are often consolidated onto a form to determine if a pursuit is worthy of an investment. We've seen all sizes and shapes of these systems, often referred to as "Go/No Go" forms. Almost all of them have a point-scoring system with weighting factors for categories under consideration. These can include:

- The firm's relevant capabilities and experience in the proposed project's technical subject
- Availability and experience of candidates to be proposed as project manager and other key positions on the team
- Number of times you have discussed this particular opportunity with the client
- Proximity to the client
- Estimated revenue and/or profit potential
- Estimated cost to pursue
- Number of contracts estimated to be awarded
- Availability of technical and marketing resources to win and perform the work (a difficult question: if you're too busy to pursue

projects, you will certainly become less busy when the work dries up; however, you must assess if you have the time to perform what is necessary to win)

- Evaluation of the "desirability" of the client (often performed separately during a client evaluation phase). This may consider such things as their payment terms, their expectations of service providers, or "ease" of working with them.

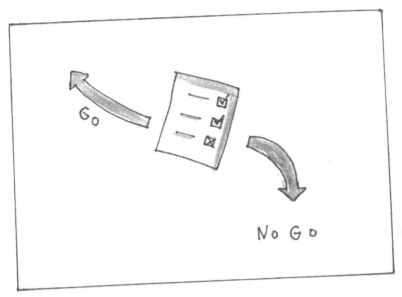

Evaluation of the scoring of rating criteria is a highly subjective judgment call. Everyone who has worked with these forms knows that the system can be manipulated to achieve the desired result, especially during a last-minute scramble over an unanticipated RFP. The Go/No Go process also often identifies numerous levels of management to approve of the decision. This can be a false indicator of agreement, since most managers would not be as informed about a pursuit as the business developers who initiated it. Unless management creates an inquisition to debate every pursuit, they must trust the people in the field to make good decisions. However, if teams seem not to win many of their pursuits, we think managers have every right to rescind this authority.

These Go/No Go forms have a definite value, and we recommend that every firm have (and use) them. But keep them in perspective. They need to be a *support* system that requests a reasoned and convincing argument for investment in a pursuit. Business Developers should be able to write a persuasive argument on why they think they can win a pursuit in about 20 minutes. Used at the last minute, they have almost no value at all. We've said many times, that if you have performed a good job in positioning, the Go/No Go decision should be a mere *formality*.

Procurement Document Distribution. It is also important in the context of decision-making to discuss the routing of procurement documents. Seems elementary, but valuable time can be wasted while RFPs make their way through a large office's mail system. If solicitations are expected from clients, then whoever is responsible for receiving and sorting mail must be on the lookout. Staff should be made aware that procurement solicitations must be pulled from the regular mail, copied, and routed to sales and marketing staff, as well as the recipient. Where this type of system is not in place, we've seen cases where RFPs have arrived, but sat quietly in the addressee's in-box while they were away on vacation.

Risk management. Because of the increasing complexity and importance of risk management to technical professional firms, we see more emphasis placed on reviewing project opportunities from a risk perspective. Management systems may include a risk committee comprised of key leadership, including senior technical, legal, and management experts. They are held responsible for safeguarding the "risk profile" of the company. Projects which have the potential to change the risk profile of a firm may include those which have construction risk, software development, or special engineering or scientific components. Certainly, design of dams, levees, tunnels, bridges, and other critical infrastructure have life safety components on which a firm must be singularly focused. In order to expedite review, the relevant risks are summarized in a system (sigh, yet another form) which can include any number of criteria such as anticipated contract provisions, commercial terms, insurance requirements, summary scope of work, estimated revenue and profit stream, and competition.

The pursuit team also must develop mitigation measures to address risks. The risk and mitigation measures are scored in much the same manner as Go/No Go decisions. A risk committee may ask questions or offer points, which can be logged into a Risk Register, for documenting a history of issues and follow-up. The Register ensures that nothing falls through the cracks, and also provides a safeguard against loss of details if project team members change (as occurs on long pursuits). The Risk Register becomes a useful reference during contract negotiations, should your firm be selected. Also, at contract signing, the Risk Register is turned over to the project management team, to be used as a starting point for managing risks throughout the life of the job.

Signature authority approval. Especially in larger firms, where pursuits can reach in the hundreds of millions of dollars, a system may be established for approving important sales commitments. These systems provide guidance on the chain of command for authority on committing the firm to a bid or proposal. The dollar value of the proposed fee can be a clear delimiter of authority, with increasing authority required for increasing dollar value of the proposal. Another criterion is to ensure sign-off by key stakeholders within the firm. For example, if a specific technical discipline is anticipated to contribute substantially to the scope of work, then their approval may be required in order to submit the proposal. Risk managers, legal or other technical approvals may be included in a signature authority "matrix."

Submittal logs. Marketing and sales personnel should track all submittals, whether competitive (bound or letter) or non-competitive (sole source). Over time, this information will allow you to evaluate your success rate, and to reveal trends. Most firms have a high success rate with letter proposals, which are often by invitation from the client. So, separating these from competitive proposals will allow more accurate measure of your success rate in the "open field." The information compiled for competitive pursuits should compare success rate from multiple perspectives, such as a firm's success rate for projects of certain sizes. In addition, you could analyze trends by geography, sector, or type of service. Another benefit of tracking this information is that you should be able to report the volume of outstanding decisions pending at any one time. We find that quarterly reports adequately provide trending patterns. Success trends for proposals submitted for a given sector, service, or geography are also important metrics. These can be helpful in justifying staffing levels for business development and marketing staff.

We recommend that your submittal log be integrated with your sales pipeline to avoid duplicating lists. If past, present, and future pursuits are maintained together, then there should be a nice flow of information from the lead phase, through submittal of proposal, and then ultimately to win or loss.

Project Information Database. One of the most important systems is one that organizes the information needed to prepare proposals and statements of qualifications. An entire book could be written on developing and implementing a database for project information. Prior to discussing the aspects of developing a system for this information, one must first understand the value of the intellectual capital of a technical services firm. Your technical teams are selling their knowledge to clients, based on what they learned in school, and also on what they learned working with clients, on the job. These project experiences are the badges by which other clients determine the level and relevance of their knowledge, a primary selection criteria. A major element of proposals and statements of qualification is to provide "proofs of knowledge to prospective clients that the team's past experience exceeds that of any competitor or is significant to be judged as competent." Therefore, a system that supports the housing of this information and sharing it across the organization should be one of your firm's top priorities.

Any marketer knows how difficult it is to get technical staff to write descriptions of their project experience, though this information is needed in nearly every sales document that a firm produces. Project sheets, statements of qualification, proposals, resumes, and other collateral are founded on project descriptions of past work history. A solid project description is priceless, so developing storage and retrieval systems for them should be an investment any firm is willing to make.

Systems for storing project information can range from hard copy file folders to server-based, custom-built software programs, depending on the size of the firm. We have learned that it is crucial to decide whether to build a stand-alone system within the marketing department or to partner with the accounting department to leverage existing information on projects. In addition, there are a multitude of technical decisions that are the realm of the IT department, another potential partner in developing a system.

No matter the sophistication of the system, the information to be gathered and stored includes:
- Project name and location
- Full description of the project
- Alternative descriptions focused on unique aspects (such as sustainability or public acceptance)
- Fee, budget, and schedule, as well as performance against these measures

- Numeric details (length of pipeline project, miles of roadway, capacity of a reservoir in gallons, size of generators, height of building)
- Reference name and phone numbers (perhaps cross-referenced with your mailing list)

There are many other details to be decided. The key is to agree on the importance of the firm's intellectual capital, then to convince management to invest in a system that takes care of this information. The results are increased efficiency in development of sales documents, no small benefit.

Systems to Track and Report Performance

There is an old adage about measuring what you intend to manage, and managing what you wish to improve. Tracking, reporting, and managing the performance of a business development program are directly related to the profitability of the firm. A firm focused on improved profitability should expect to measure performance, subdivided by departments, business lines, and individuals. We hope your firm's chief financial and information officers are your best friends. These professionals are the keepers of data which allow you to understand the performance of your enterprise.

> *It can be easy to go overboard with cost accounting. While we can measure many things, and, as we all know, technical professionals love math, we've seen many firms gravitate toward a method of managing people through budgets. We agree that having budgets is important for accountability. However, budgets do not lead people—people lead people. A firm cannot modify human behavior by managing numbers.*

It's important to keep in mind that most technical professional firms carry two sets of financial books: 1) General ledger, and 2) Project cost accounting. Both are immense sources of information and contain thousands, if not millions, of transactions. You can learn a great deal if you have the ability to run reports from simple database tools or a spreadsheet.

Recently, we're also seeing accounting software vendors adding business development features to their systems. Some marketing organizations create their own tracking and reporting systems, but these can be demanding to develop. And if your data doesn't reconcile with accounting data, then it will be suspect. So, work with accounting to develop the information you need.

Sales. This is likely the most reported statistic and we've seen it tracked, calculated, and reported in many ways. We like the simplest definition of a "sale:" backlog at end of period, less backlog at beginning of period, plus earned revenue for the period. Some firms report sales as total contract value at signing. This can be misleading because we know of many occasions in which contracts were halted midstream, or not even begun after signing, thus providing no

> In many services firms, a sale is recorded as the new contract (or amendment) is signed and booked into your accounting system. However, keep in mind that your firm doesn't earn revenue from the sale until you perform the work, you record your time on timecards, the client is invoiced and the bill is paid. This is very different from buying other services and consumer goods, in which the sale and revenues are booked and earned nearly instantaneously as you swipe your credit card.

revenue for the firm. In addition, because revenues (and hence sales) for most technical professional firms are dominated by labor charges, it is common to track by both total and net (labor) sales.

Backlog can typically be defined as the budgeted value of all booked projects, less work invoiced against the budget. In other words, it's the amount of remaining budget or workload available to the firm through authorized contracts. As with sales and revenues, backlog is often shown as total and net (labor). Backlog is also often expressed as months of work remaining at the current average revenue earn rate.

Indirect cost management. Tracking your marketing spending is an essential means of managing your program against a budget. By establishing cost budgets for selected activities, your project cost accounting system will allow managers to monitor and control costs. Breaking your business development program down by activity will allow you to establish individual budgets, track costs (expenses for labor and other items) and make changes in mid-stream should you find your program over- or under-investing in a given area. Suggested activities for assigning budgets include:

- Client contact and prospecting
- Pursuits (including capture planning and positioning)
- Proposal and interview preparation

- Negotiations
- External activities, such as conferences and committees
- Internal development activities, such as preparation of collateral
- Corporate communication and advertising

BD Ratio. This is a simple quotient of: a) a firm's sales, divided by b) the cost of marketing those sales. This can be calculated in any category you wish to actively manage. It's a useful means of monitoring the effect of every dollar invested in sales.

Success Rate. This is also a common metric for business development (also referred to as hit rate). By tracking submittals and identifying wins and losses, a percent success rate can be calculated. Many firms further break this down by competitive and non-competitive submittals. It may be worthwhile to calculate success rate based on the dollar value of the submittals and the number of submittals. Even finer granularity can be achieved if you track success on projects over a certain size—to assess your ability to close sales of increasing complexity.

Pipeline Size. It is helpful to know the volume of potential work you are tracking (your Pipeline) as a measure of the size of the market to which you have access. By tracking potential pursuits over time, you can assess market trends, particularly in tough times. Admittedly, this is one of the fuzziest metrics of all – subject to a multitude of uncertainties because of the difficult nature of accurately quantifying opportunities. Nonetheless, with a little diligence in breaking down the pipeline by geography and market sector, important trends can be discerned.

Once you have decided upon key metrics for monitoring the performance of your business development organization, then reports can be designed for presenting details, summaries, and analyses to the leaders of your firm. Reporting on the results of individuals responsible for business development can be helpful if your performance metric incorporate individual sales goals. Remember, only measure what you intend to manage.

Systems for Managing Other External activities

Many firms develop a system to organize their external activities (covered in our Chapter on Effective Conference and Trade Show Attendance) to get noticed by potential clients, including:

- Conference and trade shows
- Participation in professional societies and committee membership
- Client social events, such as dinners and sporting events.

In some firms, these activities and responsibilities can be planned (and tracked) at any level of detail. In our view, the level of detail can be scaled up or down depending on the amount of attention you need to pay on the nature and degree of investment. We find that some firms can grow out of balance over time between these types of external activities and good old-fashioned, face-to-face client contacts. If this is the case, then more detail is appropriate to maintain a budget that is balanced against the overall business development budget.

To achieve value from an investment in conferences or other group events, it's important to track and regularly monitor attendance and follow-through. This will help you see which activities should be sustained, and which ones may have sounded like a good idea, but do not provide the intended results. Establishing budgets will also help immensely with accountability. This tool helps marketing staff who are asked to provide support for arrangements that require advance planning.

We recommend two additional systems to leverage value from external activities. The first is to institute a formal approval framework. This may meet with initial resistance from technical professional staff, but explaining the need to meet budgets and achieve profitability goals goes a long ways toward adoption. Your accounting department can also make reimbursement of expenses for conference attendance contingent upon having an approval on file. The second system is to require each attendee to provide a brief report on their activities at the external event to distribute new knowledge across the firm. Conference attendance reports can also produce new leads, which should be passed along to the business development team.

By requiring staff to report their activities and findings, there is a subtle but strong incentive to make the most from the time spent outside the office. We have heard far too many stories of external events where the attendee declares the conference as unrewarding. If so, then this should be taken into consideration when planning to attend again in the future. However, by insisting on the report, we find that attendees are more productive because they know they need to find a valuable experience on which to report.

Systems for BD Planning

Marketing and sales people are inevitably involved in overall company planning because of the forward-looking nature of business development. For effective business development planning, you must establish clear objectives, numeric goals, strategies, and actions. Obviously, these should be derived from your company's strategic plan, which sets the stage with an overarching vision of the direction of the company. By working with your finance department and executive management, budgets are established which lead to resource and staffing levels. Summaries can be organized for specific organizations to support management decisions on invests. As an outgrowth of this process, business development can take the lead in formulating strategies for moving into new geographies or business lines. It is often helpful to conduct a SWOT (strengths, weaknesses, opportunities and threats) analysis as a basis for strategic thinking.

Systems Management

We're not the experts on systems management, but we have learned a few things the hard way. There will always be a healthy dynamic tension between centralized and distributed philosophies and nowhere is this more prevalent than in business development. Many marketers create their own lists of opportunities and clients. While these are fine for startups, over time they create inefficiencies and impede coordination when a firm tries to act as a team.

We believe that information should be stored in one place, but with enough flexibility to offer benefits to all users. In so doing, each portion of the overall organization takes responsibility for entering data and for the quality of the information. Centralized data storage avoids the pitfalls and inefficiencies associated with duplicate information. Business development organizations should be hands-on, enthusiastic supporters of systems management. Leadership must set the example by working to ensure data is accurate and that meaningful reports are produced on a regular basis.

In summary, while support systems can help usher in change, they are not vehicles for leading change. If we focus on the "why" of a system, and less on "how," then we can determine if they are useful tools in implementing a marketing and sales program.

We explained to our colleague that Go/No Go forms were not bureaucratic paperwork to be filled out and preserved forever like the tags on mattresses. They were in-

struments to support making decisions on whether or not to pursue opportunities. In our view, compiling a library of completed forms was not the point. The point is to provide sales systems that increase the chances of winning targeted opportunities by clarifying whether the pursuit is viable and that you have a strong chance of winning, by the nature of your responses to the form's questions. Completing the form becomes a formality when the proper discussions and inquiries have taken place.

"We were told by Corporate that these things needed to be filled out and kept, now are you telling us we don't need to?"

"This isn't about the forms. Do you complete Quality Assurance forms for the sake of marking a checklist? No, it's because you derive value from the process."

"Then we don't have to save them anymore?"

"Come with us outside. We'll have a bonfire."

Chapter 10
Annotated Bibliography

*"It is a good thing for an uneducated man to read
good books of quotations."*
– Winston Churchill

1.   Beckwith, Harry. *Selling the Invisible: A Field Guide to Modern Marketing*. New York: Warner, 1997. Print. One of the first books to address the under-discussed topic of sales within the services industry. There are a surprising number of tricks of the trade which can be applied to the sales of rocket science.

2.   "Brand." *Wikipedia*. Wikimedia Foundation, 22 Apr. 2014. Web. 22 Apr. 2014. A solid description of a difficult concept.

3.   Cohen, Herb. *You Can Negotiate Anything*. Secaucus, NJ: L. Stuart, 1980. Print. This lays a concrete foundation on building negotiating skills.

4.   Collins, James C. *Good to Great: Why Some Companies Make the Leap--and Others Don't*. New York, NY: Harper Business, 2001. Print. Knowing who to "get on the bus" is key to forming any successful team. The makeup of your sales team, both technical and marketers, is crucial to achieving your business development goals. This book shows how the great firms accomplish it.

5.   Covey, Sean. *The 7 Habits of Highly Effective Teens: The Miniature Edition: The Ultimate Teenage Success Guide*. Philadelphia: Running, 2002. Print. Helpful for people of any age.

6.   Davidow, William H., and Bro Uttal. *Total Customer Service: The Ultimate Weapon*. New York: Harper & Row, 1989. Print. One of the early books to pick up on the power of superior customer service in improving performance and your bottom line.

7.   Donaldson, Michael C. *Fearless Negotiating: The Wish-want-walk Method to Reach Solutions That Work*. New York: McGraw-Hill, 2007. Print. The W-W-W method is compelling.

8. Gladwell, Malcolm. *The Tipping Point: How Little Things Can Make a Big Difference*. Boston: Little, Brown, 2000. Print. At first, this book seems more of an explanation of pop culture than applicable to business, but it offers a number of new perspectives on how little things become big. Written before the phrase "going viral" was popularized. We like the explanation of connectors, mavens, and salesmen.

9. Goleman, Daniel, Richard E. Boyatzis, and Annie McKee. *Primal Leadership: Realizing the Power of Emotional Intelligence*. Boston, MA: Harvard Business School, 2002. Print. An important argument in favor of emotions in the business environment. Compares intelligence quotient (IQ) versus the emotional intelligence (EQ) of leaders and their impact on people, organizations, and culture.

10. Green, Charles H. *Trust-based Selling: Using Customer Focus and Collaboration to Build Long-term Relationships*. New York: McGraw-Hill, 2006. Print. By one of the authors of *The Trusted Advisor*, this book takes the concept of selling through trust relationships one step further. As you read this and begin to think about the examples, you'll have that feeling of déjà vu over those extraordinarily successful people you know in the business.

11. Greenleaf, Robert K. *Servant Leadership: A Journey into the Nature of Legitimate Power and Greatness*. New York: Paulist, 1977. Print. Greenleaf's 1970 essay "The Servant as Leader" followed by the book in 1977 were seminal works. One of the best philosophical, almost spiritual, books on how to get people to do the right thing.

12. Heath, Chip, and Dan Heath. *Switch: How to Change Things When Change Is Hard*. New York: Broadway, 2010. Print. We really liked the explanation of how to motivate the feelings (art) of your customers in comparison to their analytical (rocket science) direction. For technology based companies, the authors' tips on managing change when all else fails are spot on.

13. Heskett, James L. *Managing in the Service Economy*. Boston, MA: Harvard Business School, 1986. Print. This is a nice overall look at how to manage a services firm, as opposed to a manufacturing operation. While many business books deal with Fortune 500 or 1000 companies who make products, this book talks about serving something to clients.

14. Hesse, Hermann. *The Journey to the East*. New York: Noonday, 1957. Print. Go ahead, read it, it won't hurt you.

15. Kaplan, Robert S.; Norton, David P., *The Balanced Scorecard*, Harvard Business School Press, 1996. Print. While this doesn't directly apply to business development, sooner or later your management is likely to bring one of these to the table. You should be ready and know what is expected of you in doing your part for the overall company's success.

16. Kim, W. Chan., and Renée Mauborgne. *Blue Ocean Strategy: How to Create Uncontested Market Space and Make the Competition Irrelevant*. Boston, MA: Harvard Business School, 2005. Print. Do you find your technologists looking to copy the competition? Is there a market leader they're trying to imitate? Consider going where the competition isn't and creating a new market where you can be first.

17. Kotter, John P. *Leading Change*. Boston, MA: Harvard Business School, 1996. Print. Over the years, we've probably referred to this book for getting things done more often than any other book. It's a primer on how to change your business to meet new competitive demands in the market place.

18. Maister, David H., Charles H. Green, and Robert M. Galford. *The Trusted Advisor*. New York: Free, 2000. Print. We are often asked if there were only one relevant book to read, what would we recommend? This book is it. More than any other book, The Trusted Advisor bridges the gap between simply solving your client's problems to becoming one of their inner circle of advisors. If you can truly understand the nature of superior professional relationships, then you'll be ahead of the pack in balancing art with rocket science.

19. Maister, David. *Managing the Professional Service Firm*. London: Free Business, 2003. Print. By one of the authors of The Trusted Advisor. It is one of the few books which take an analytical look at successful models for organizing and running a consulting firm. Most business books focus on large manufacturing or non-professional service companies.

20. Merrill, David W., and Roger H. Reid. *Personal Styles & Effective Performance*. Radnor, PA: Chilton Book, 1981. Print. These authors delve into basic personality types and the characteristics of behav-

ior. More importantly, they lay the foundation for approaching the art of persuading each personality type, as they are decidedly different from one another.

21. Miller, Arthur. *Death of a Salesman*. New York: Penguin, 1996. Print. Goes without saying, a classic.

22. Naisbitt, John. *Megatrends: Ten New Directions Transforming Our Lives*. New York: Warner, 1982. Print. This is an oldie but goodie and offers insights to the future. It is surprising how many of these predictions came true (and how many did not). Nonetheless, it is a worthwhile exercise in thinking ahead of your market place and planning accordingly.

23. Potter, Robert A. *Winning in the Invisible Market: A Guide to Selling Professional Services in the Turbulent times*. United States: R.A. Potter, 2003. Print. One of the first authors to recognize the abstract nature of services, and how sales must be approached differently than for consumer goods and non-technical services.

24. Rose, Stuart W. *Mandeville: A Guide for the Marketing of Professional Services*. Washington, D.C.: Professional Development Resources, 1995. Print. Expert book on the art of listening.

25. Sun Tzu, and Samuel B. Griffith. *The Art of War*. London: Oxford UP, 1971. Print. Popularized in the movie Wall Street, this book has been reprinted many times. It's a short, but worthwhile read of some ancient concepts which still apply to competing in today's markets.

26. Surowiecki, James. *The Wisdom of Crowds: Why the Many Are Smarter than the Few and How Collective Wisdom Shapes Business, Economies, Societies, and Nations*. New York: Doubleday, 2004. Print. If you're either looking to sell to a large market or trying to understand an internal issue, read this book. It does a nice job of explaining how two (or many more) heads are better than one.

27. Weitz, Barton A. "Effectiveness in Sales Interactions: A Contingency Framework." *Journal of Marketing* 45.1 (1981): 85. Print.

28. Weitz, Barton A., Harish Sujan, and Mita Sujan. "Knowledge, Motivation, and Adaptive Behavior: A Framework for Improving Selling Effectiveness." *Journal of Marketing* 50.4 (1986): 174. Print.

ABOUT THE AUTHORS

Charles McIntyre is Director of Marketing for an electrical and technology construction firm. He has worked in the technical professional services industry for more than 20 years, and is a member of the Society of Marketing Professional Services (SMPS). As a non-technical professional in a highly technical world, he bridges the gap between the art of persuasion and the science of technical solutions.

Harold Glaser is Director of Client Excellence with an engineering and environmental science firm. As a consultant, he has worked with some of the largest utilities and agencies in the world. With over 30 years of experience as a civil engineer, the emphasis of his career has been on business development. He is a Registered Professional Engineer, Life Member of the American Water Works Association, and a Member of the American Society of Civil Engineers.

Made in the USA
Las Vegas, NV
04 June 2021

24174601R00095